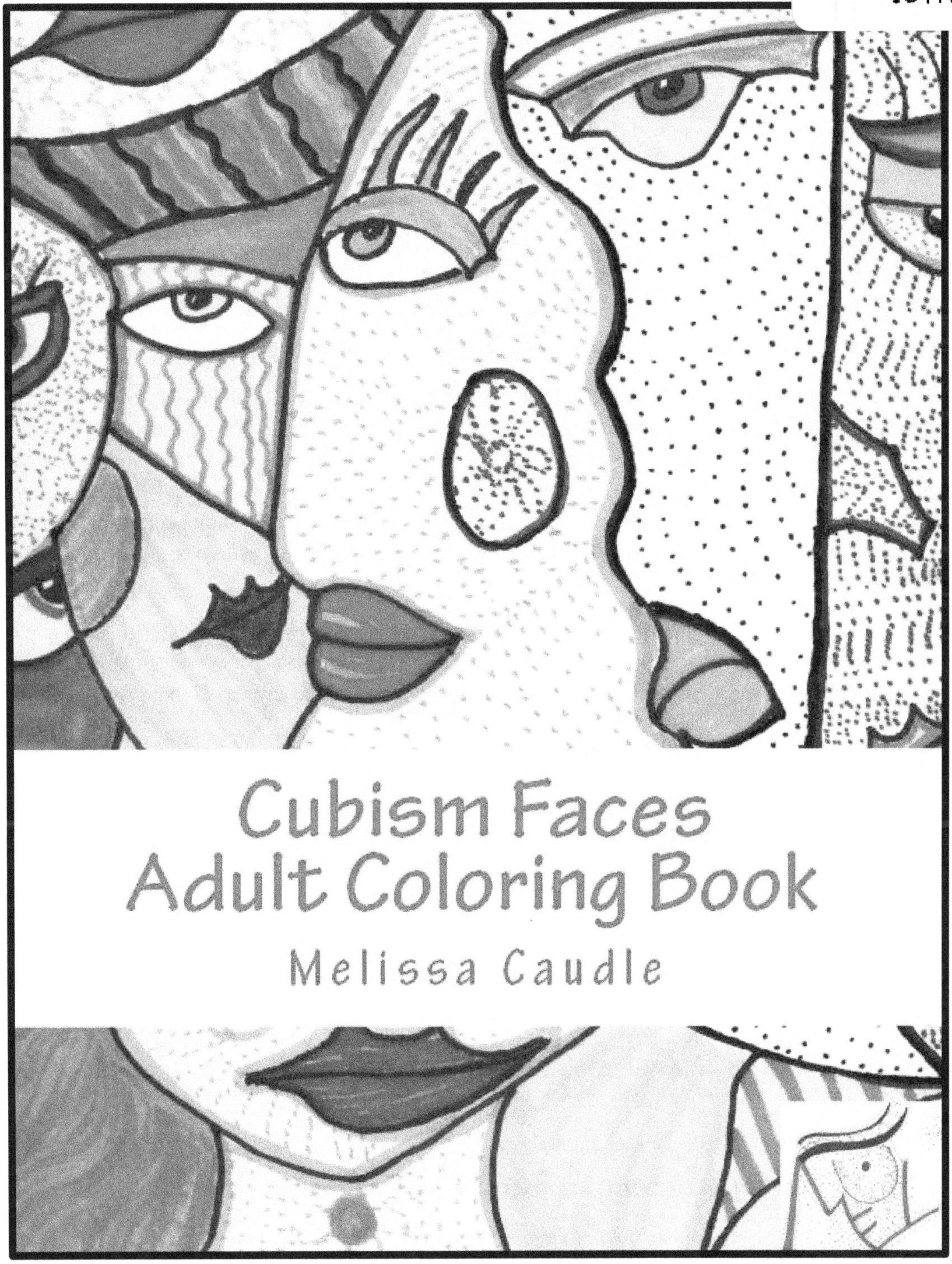

Cubism Faces
Adult Coloring Book

Melissa Caudle

OPEN DOOR PUBLISHING

NEW ORLEANS, LA

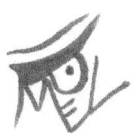

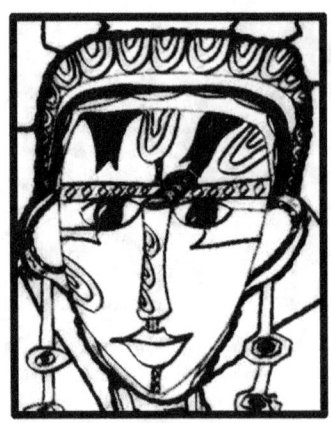

Cubism Faces an abstract art collection by artist Melissa Caudle that continues the unique drawings in her first five adult coloring book collection; but all Picasso style. Embrace each face and the inner beauty they behold as you bring life with your touch. Each one is limitless in opportunity. Use your imagination as you create your own tangles, zendangles, dots, flowers etc. I love to create patterns with dots to vary larger white spaces. That is one of my own signature pattern in my original art as seen on the front cover. Simply relax and enjoy yourself and embrace the calming effect of coloring. It really is art therapy at its best. You have complete freedom to express yourself. There is only one rule for a colorist – there are no rules.

The artist strongly advises to put a piece of cardstock or file folder behind each page as you color to avoid bleed through. As a reminder, the higher quality of marker you use, bleed through occurs. That's means the marker is doing the job of saturation and is very normal. In fact, that is what you want to happen for bold and beautiful colors.

Each drawing is printed on one side with enough margin and an outline making them suitable for framing by cutting them from the book. Lastly, several of the artist's originals, completely colored are for sale at www.drmelissacaudle.com and on E-bay. These originals come with a Certificate of Authenticity signed by the artist - an art collector's dream come true as they increase in value because of their publication in this book.

Bibliographical Note

Abstract Faces Vol I Coloring Book is a new work created by artist, Melissa Caudle. Her art is for sell on E-bay. To obtain original pieces of her, contact the artist at: melabstractart@gmail.com. She is also available for commissioned pieces.

www.drmelissacaudle.com   melabstractart@gmail.com   drmelcaudle@icloud.com

JOIN FACEBOOK: ABSTRACT FACES ADULT COLORING BOOKS

(Share your finished pages with other members of the group.)

INTERNATIONAL STANDARD BOOK NUMBER

ISBN-13: 978-1542949484   ISBN-10:1542949483

Manufactured in the United States by CreateSpace 2017

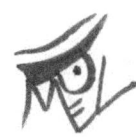

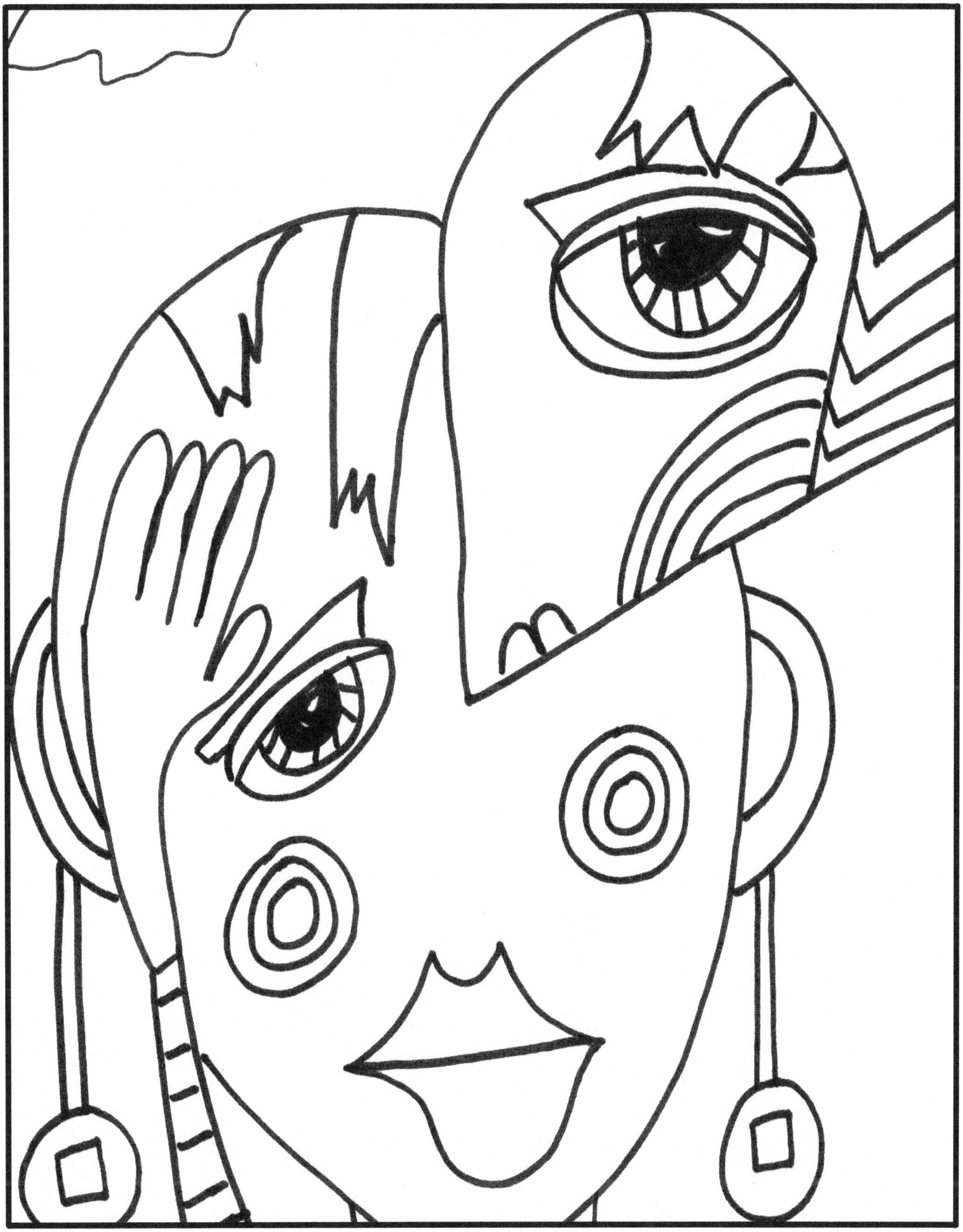

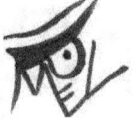

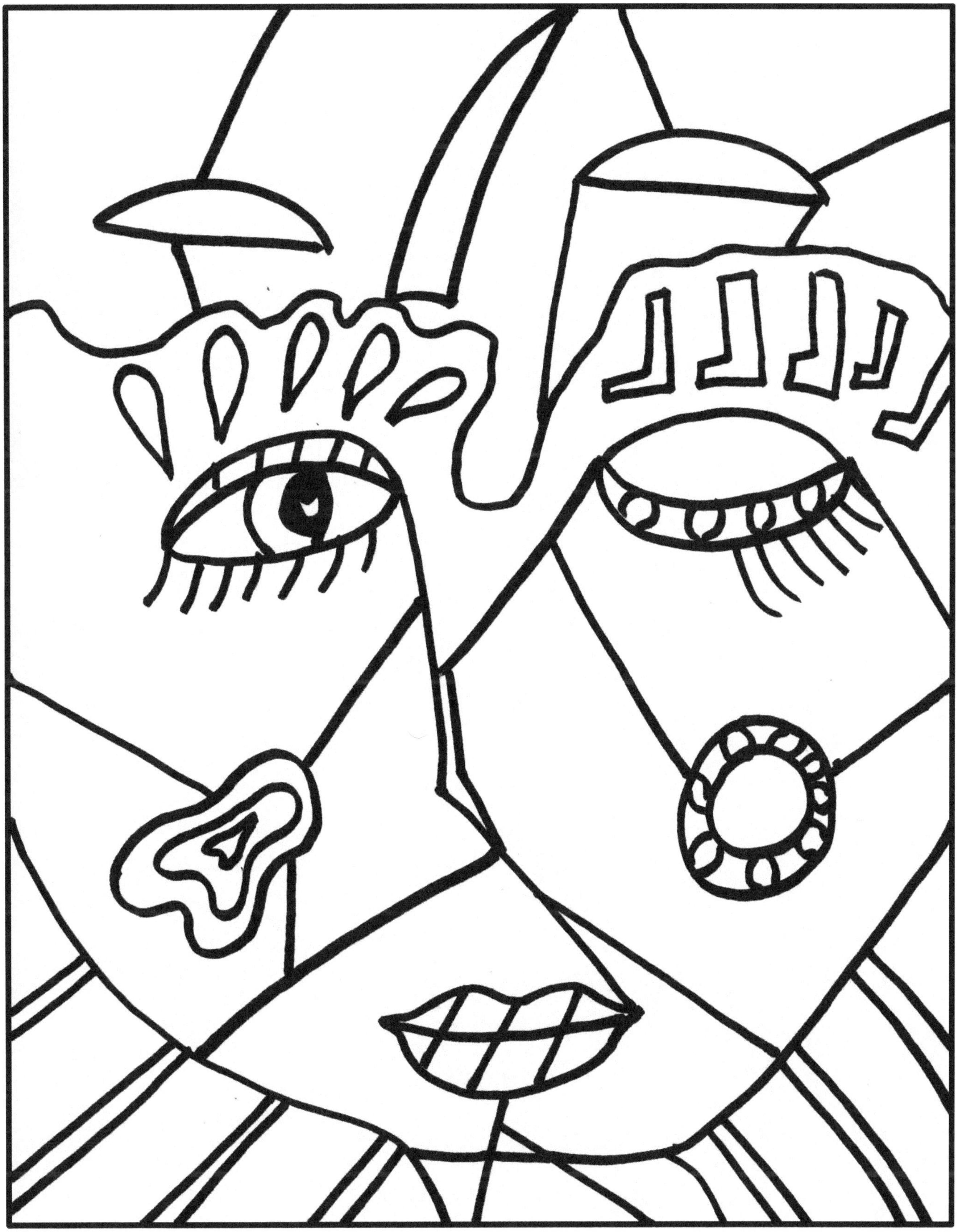

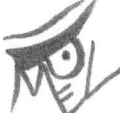

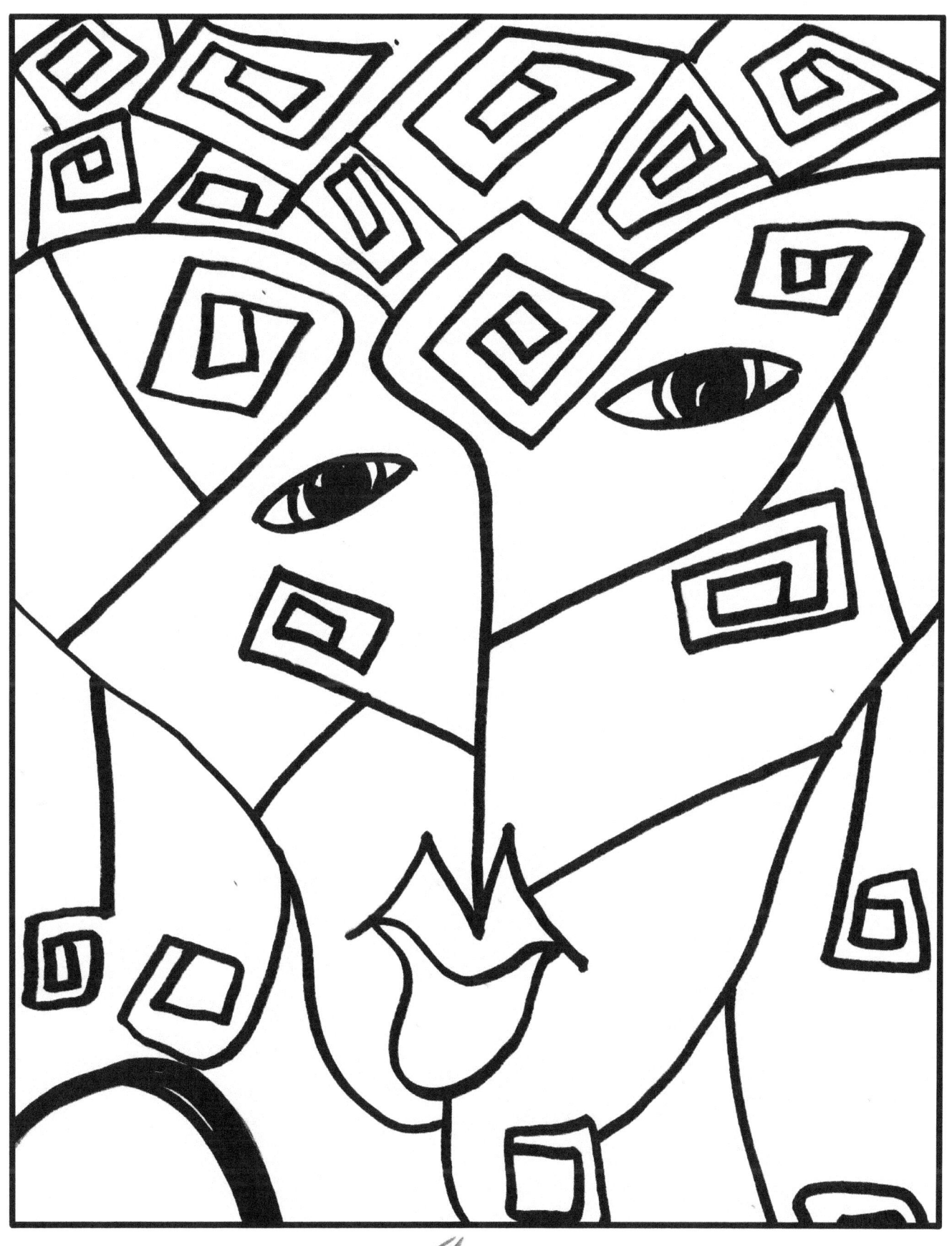

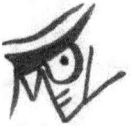

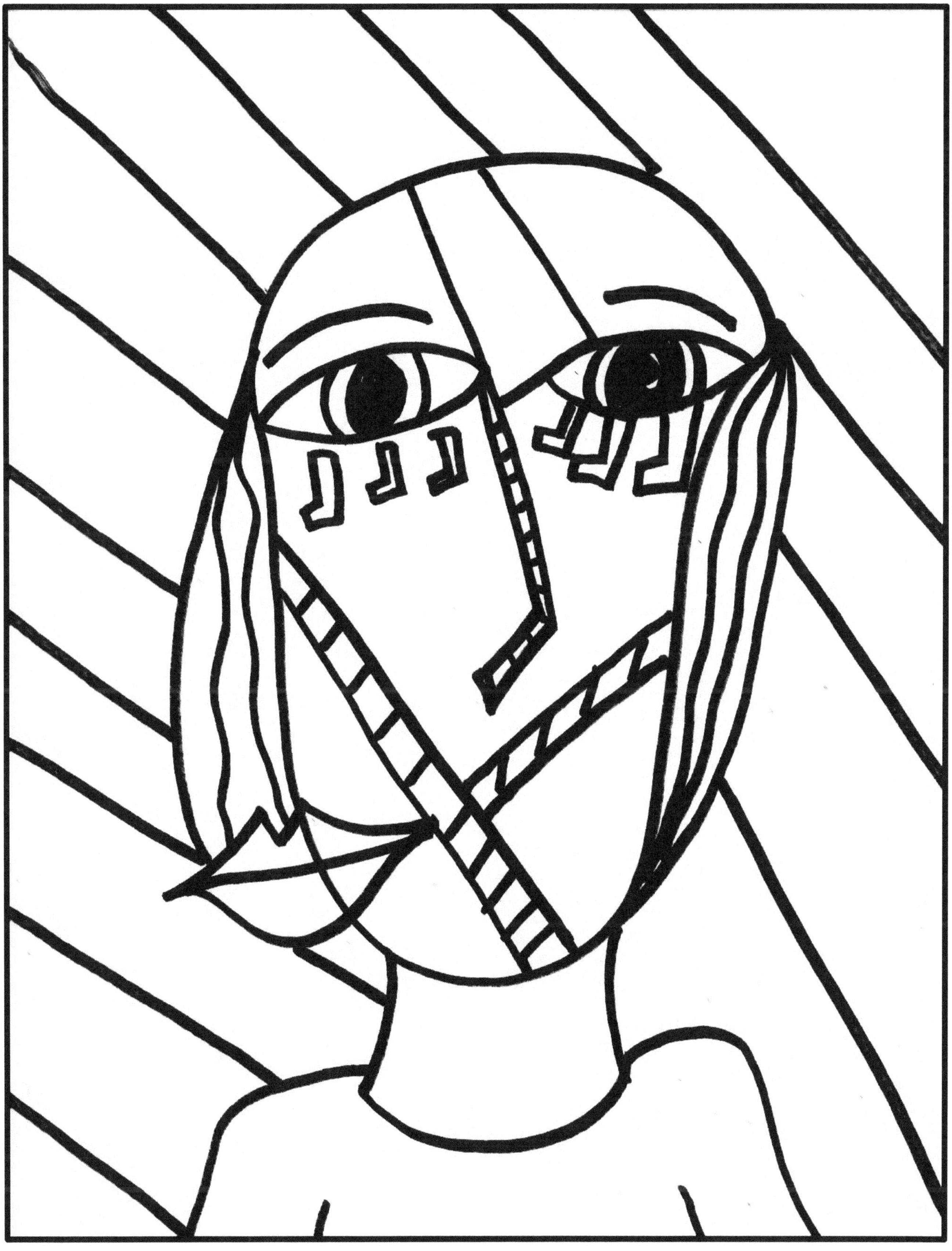

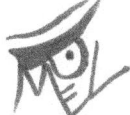

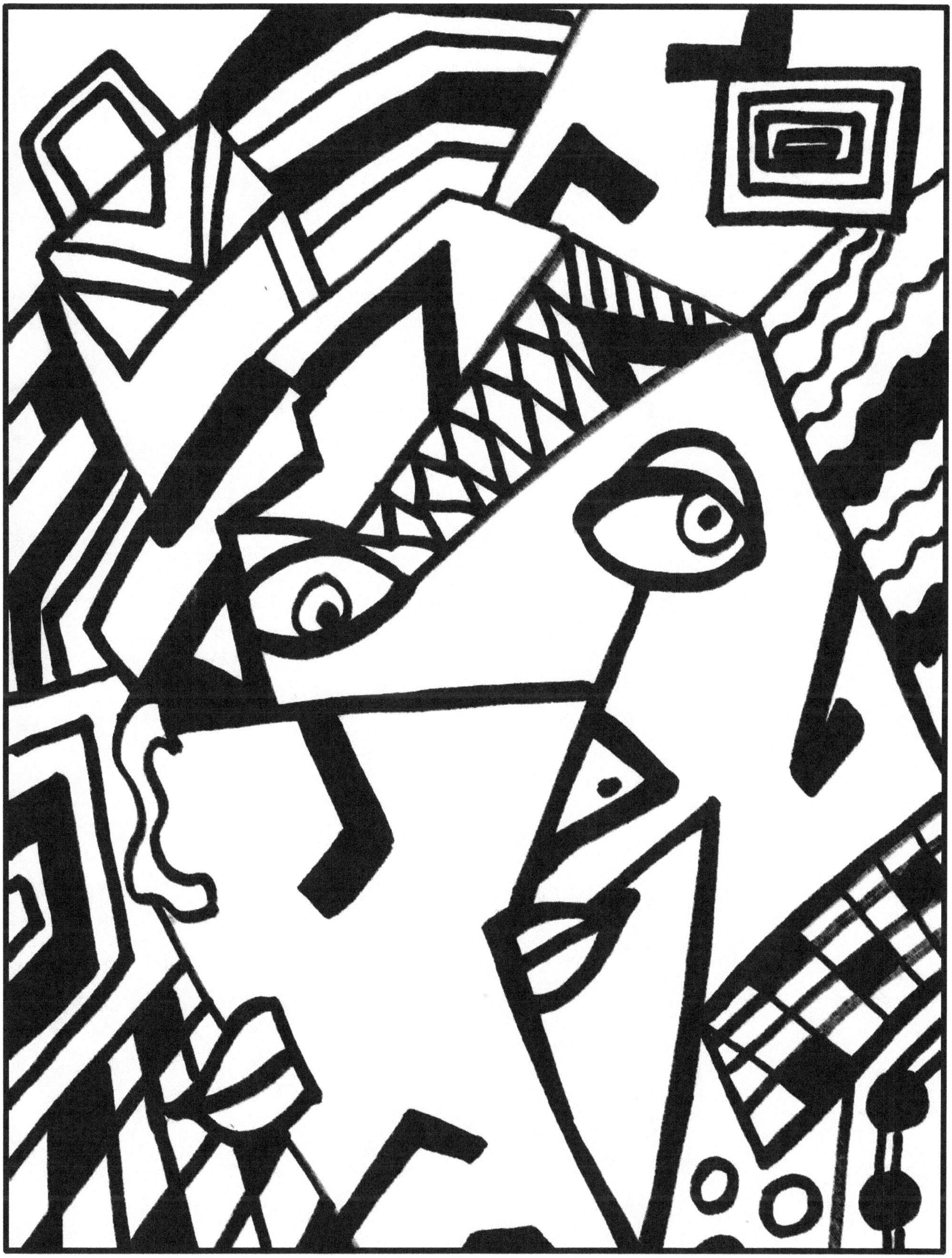

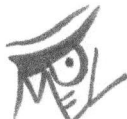

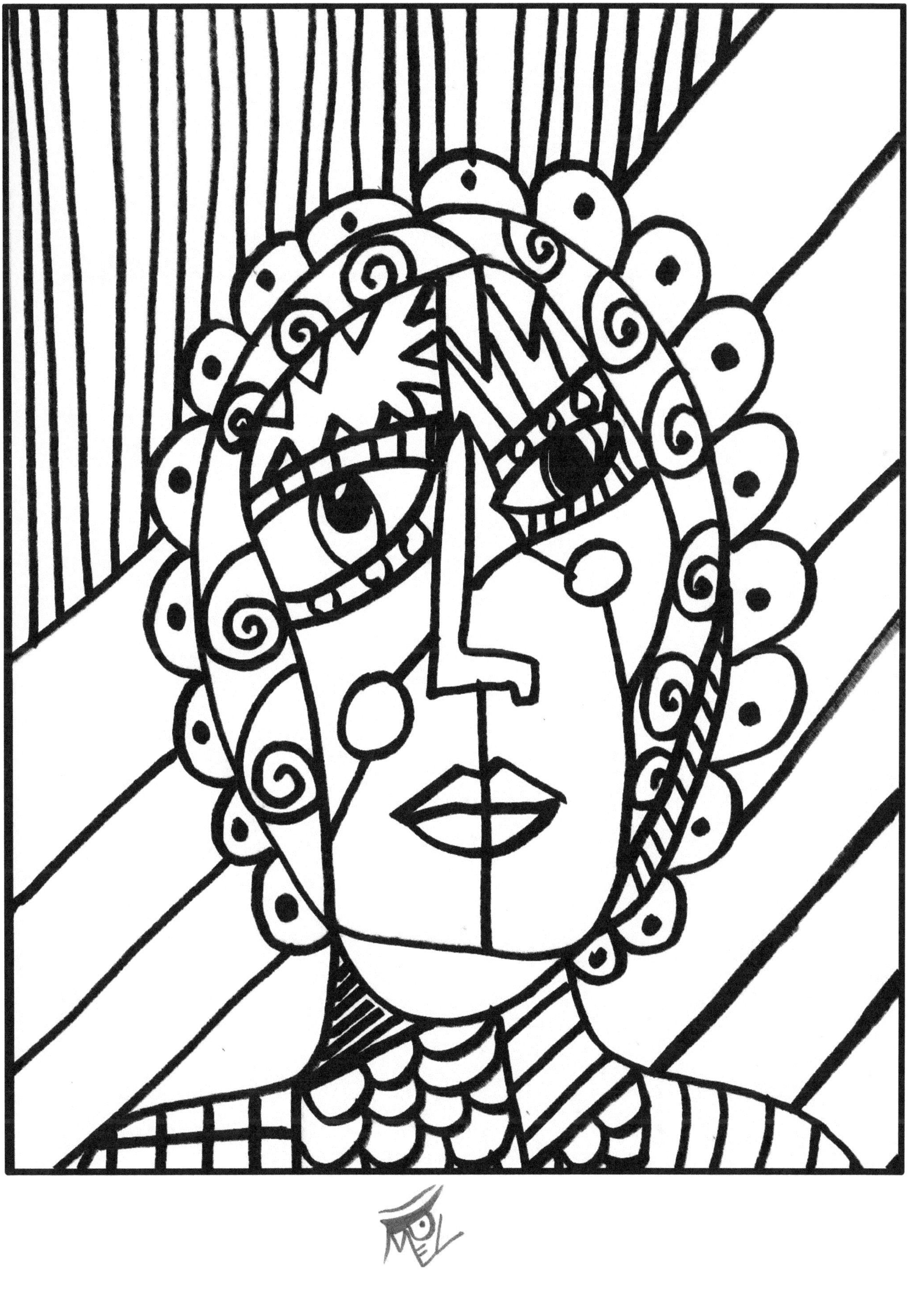

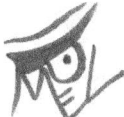

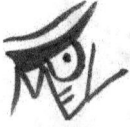

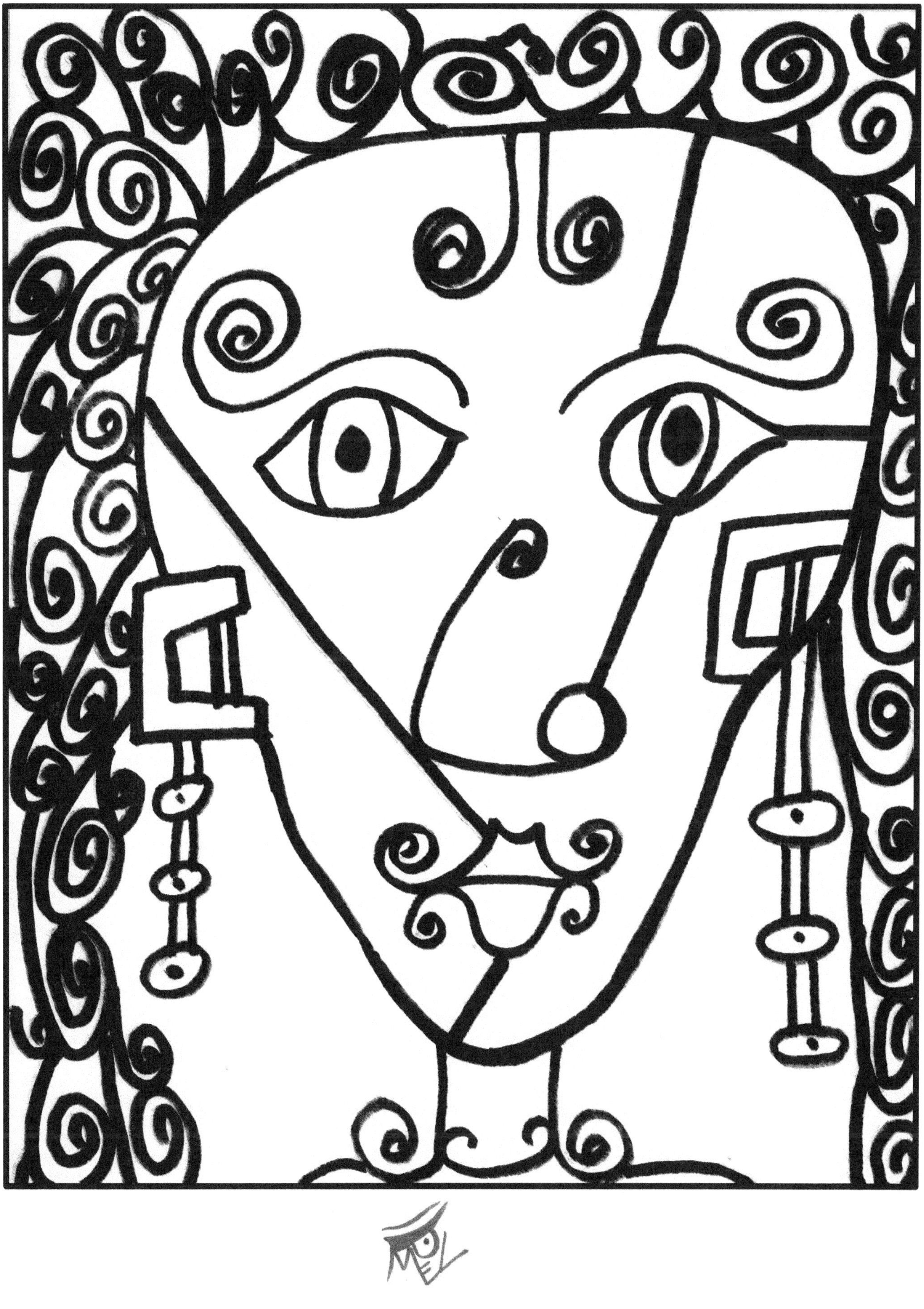

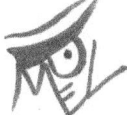

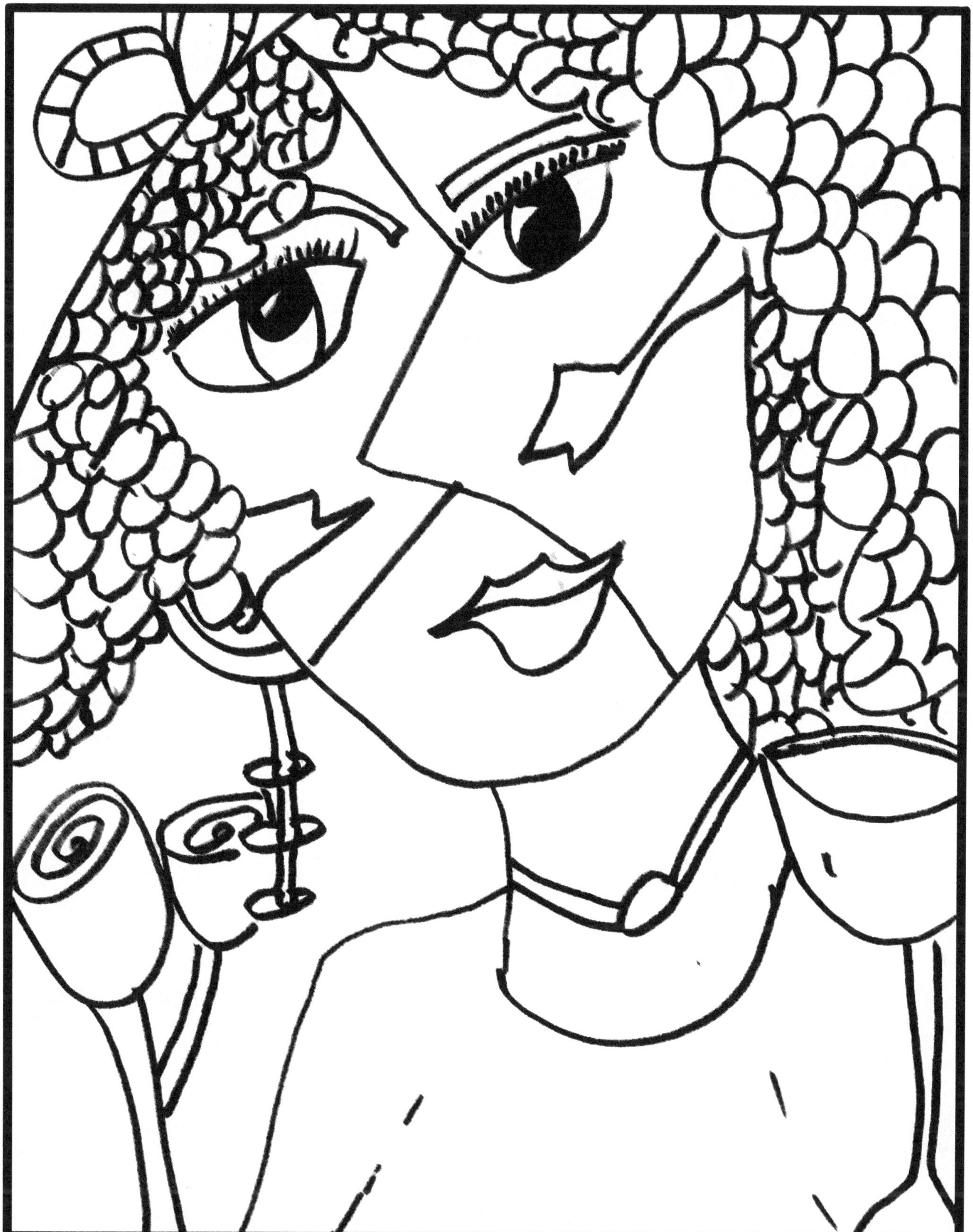

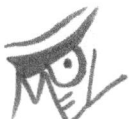

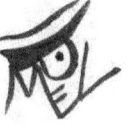

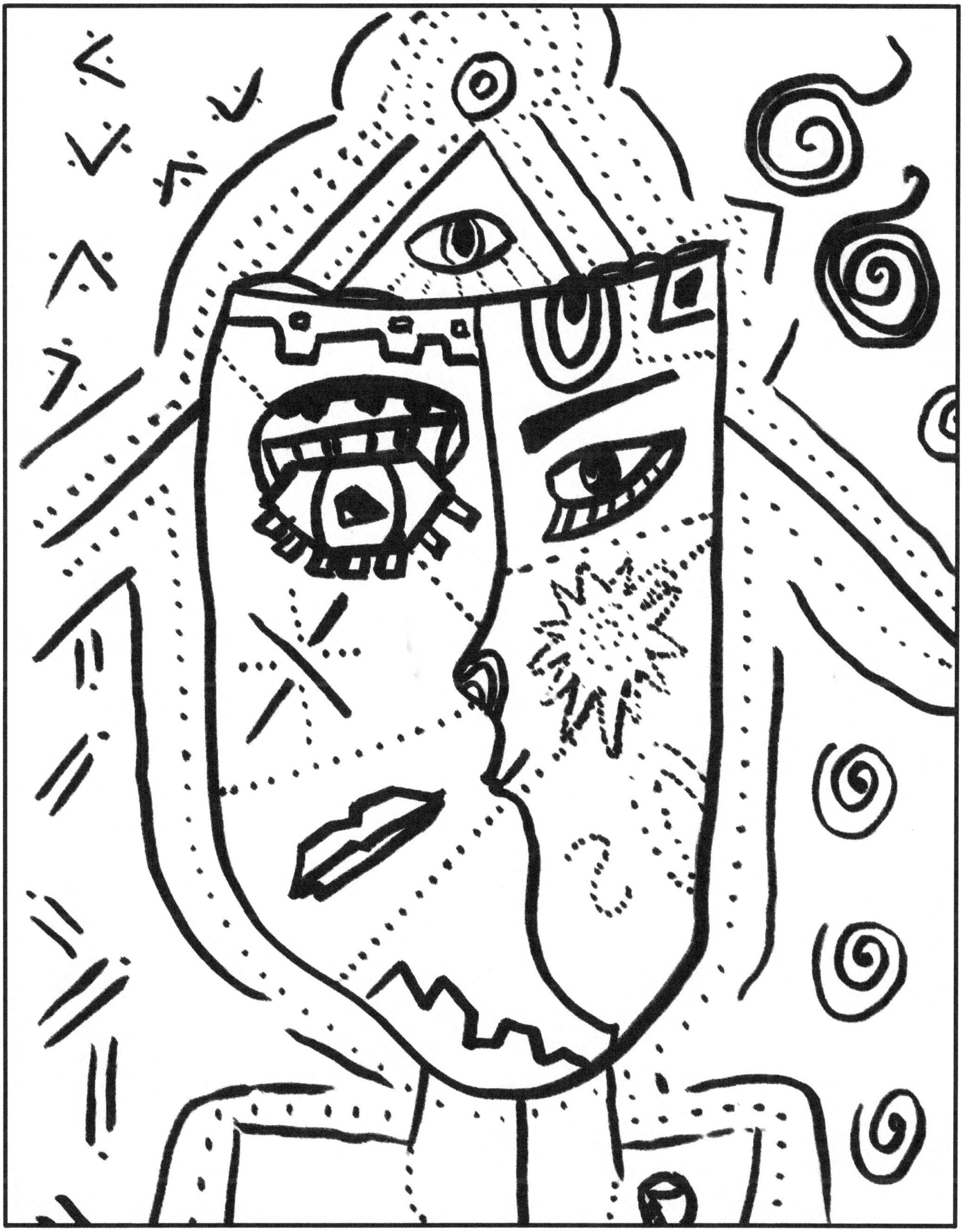

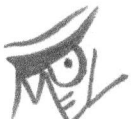

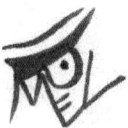

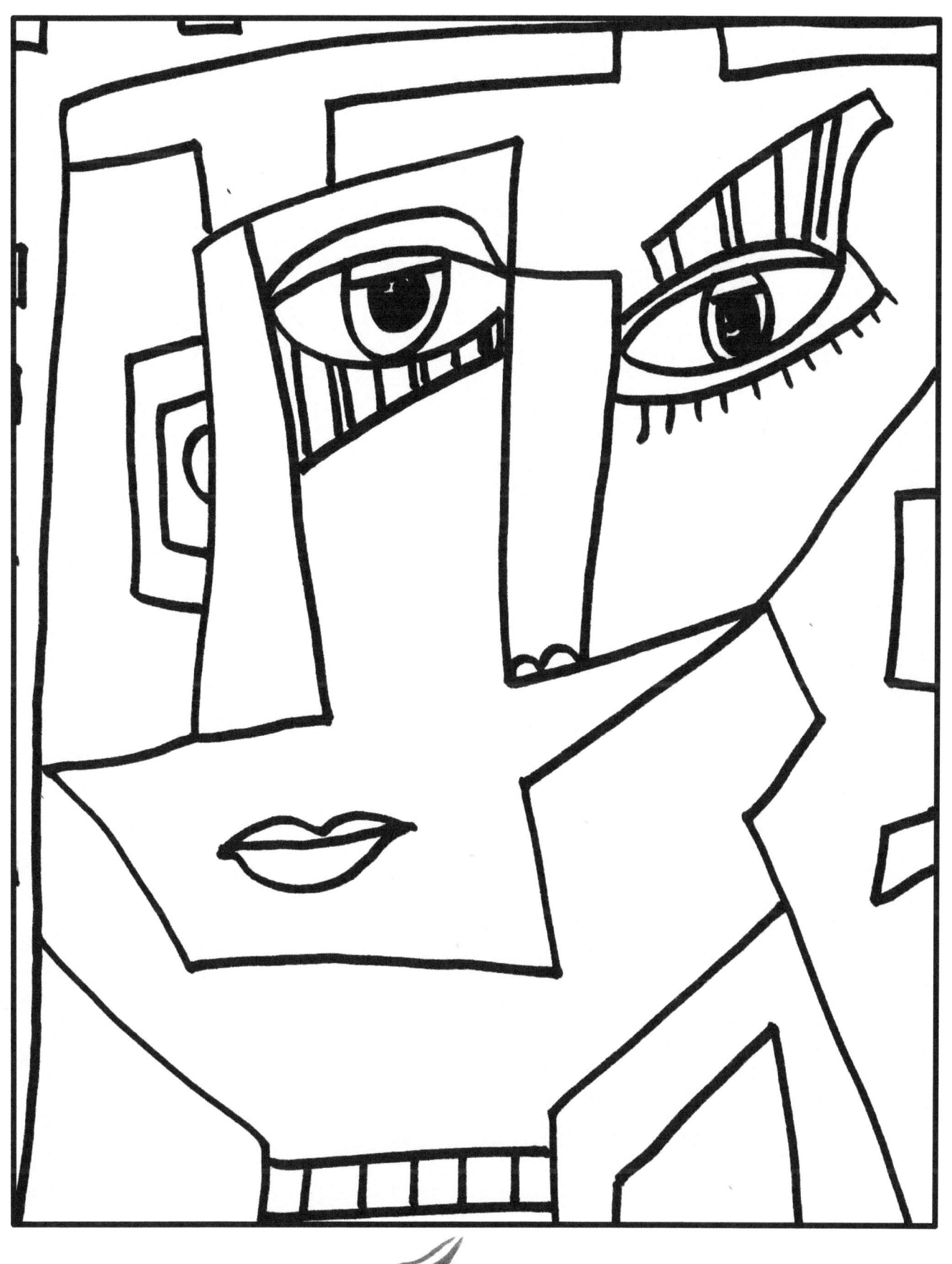

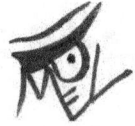

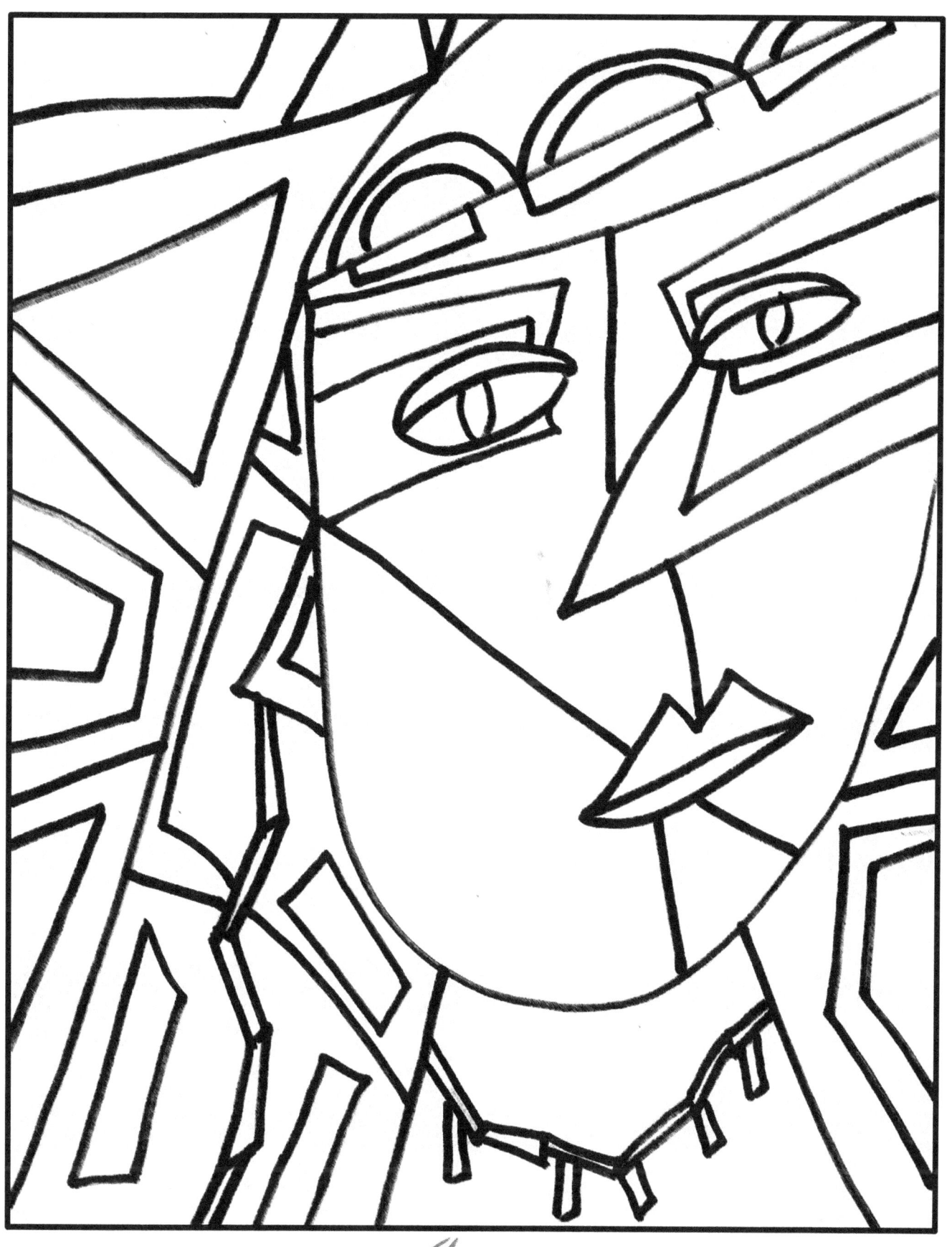

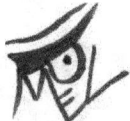

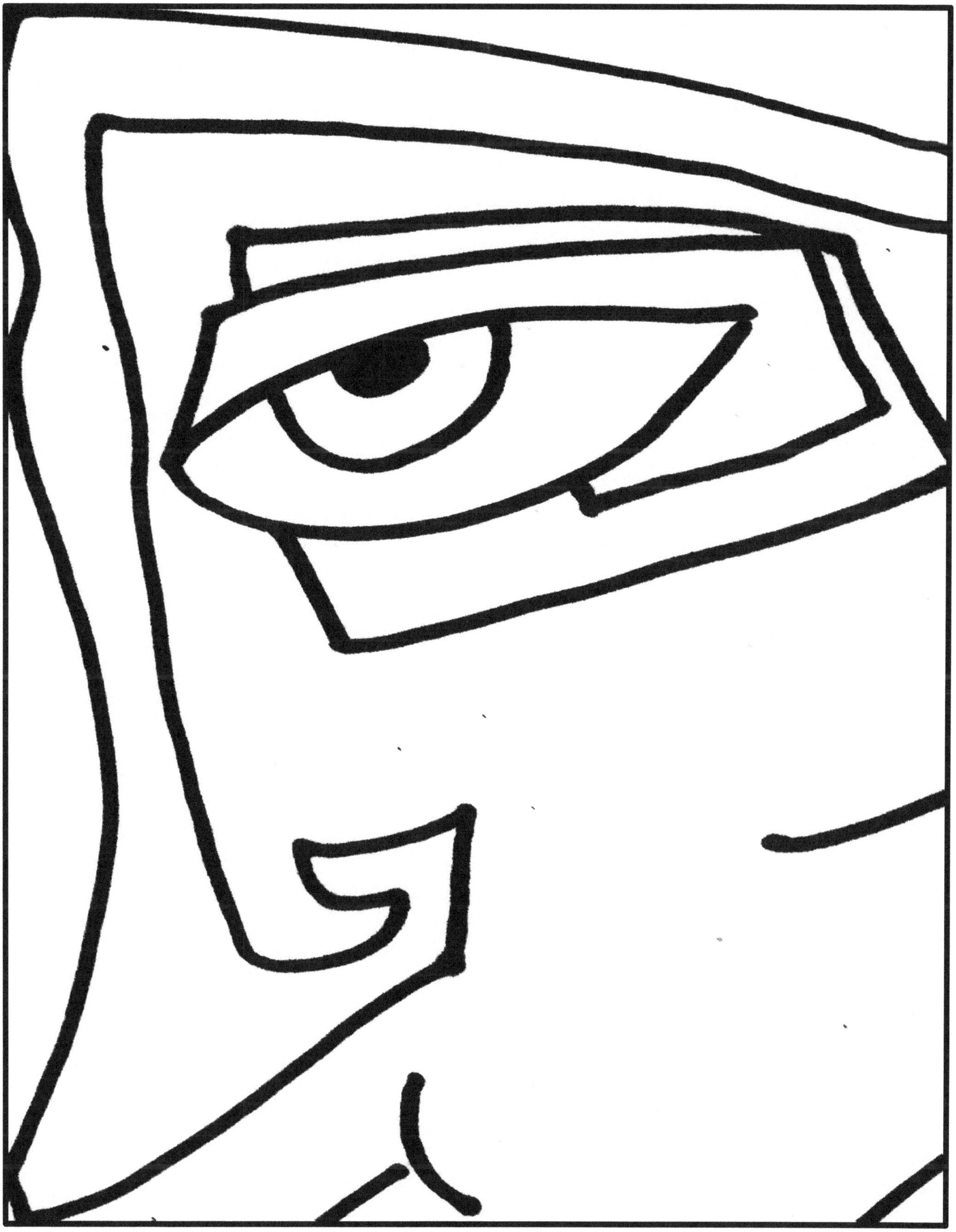

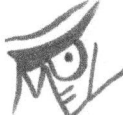

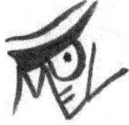

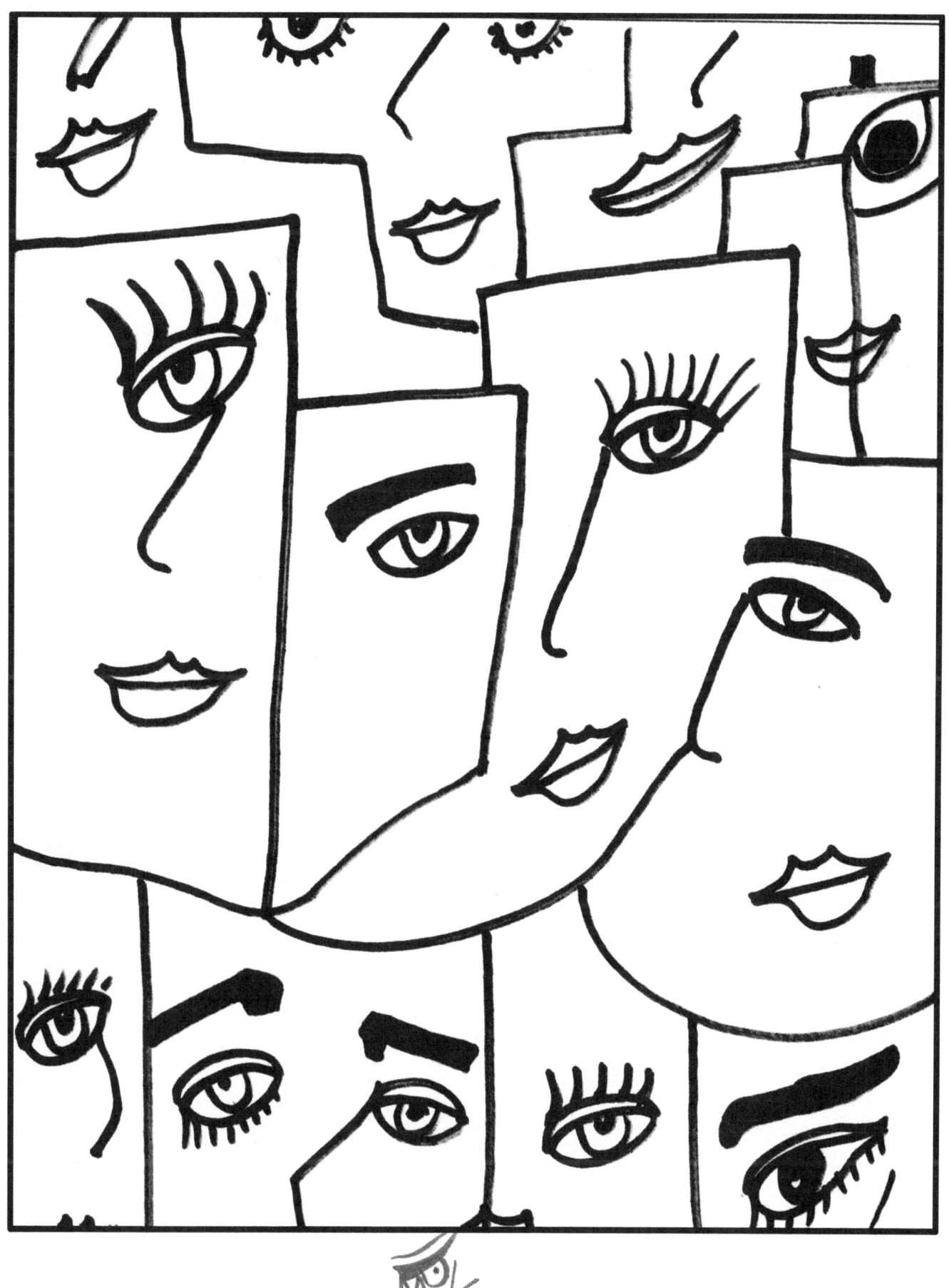

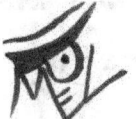

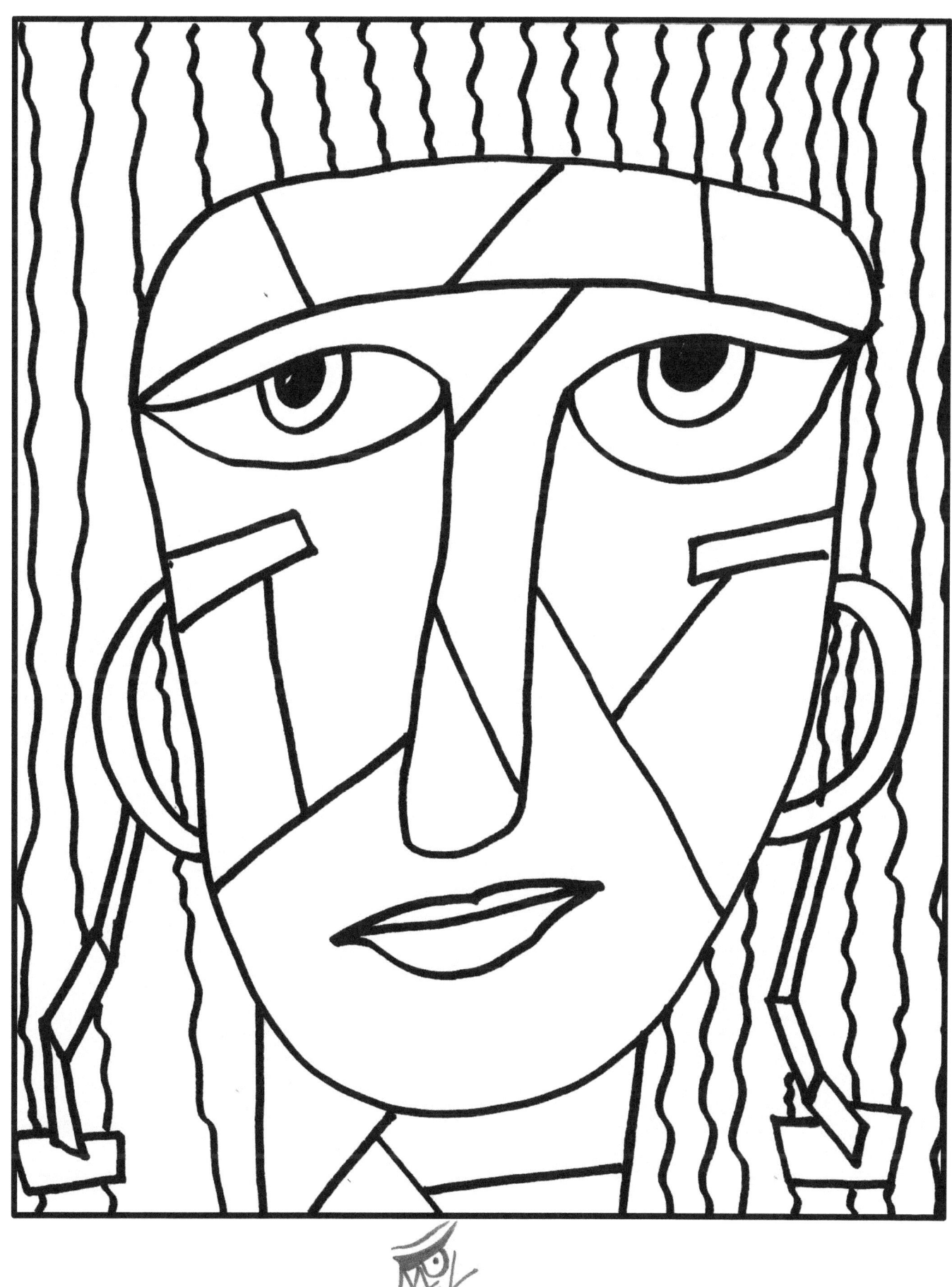

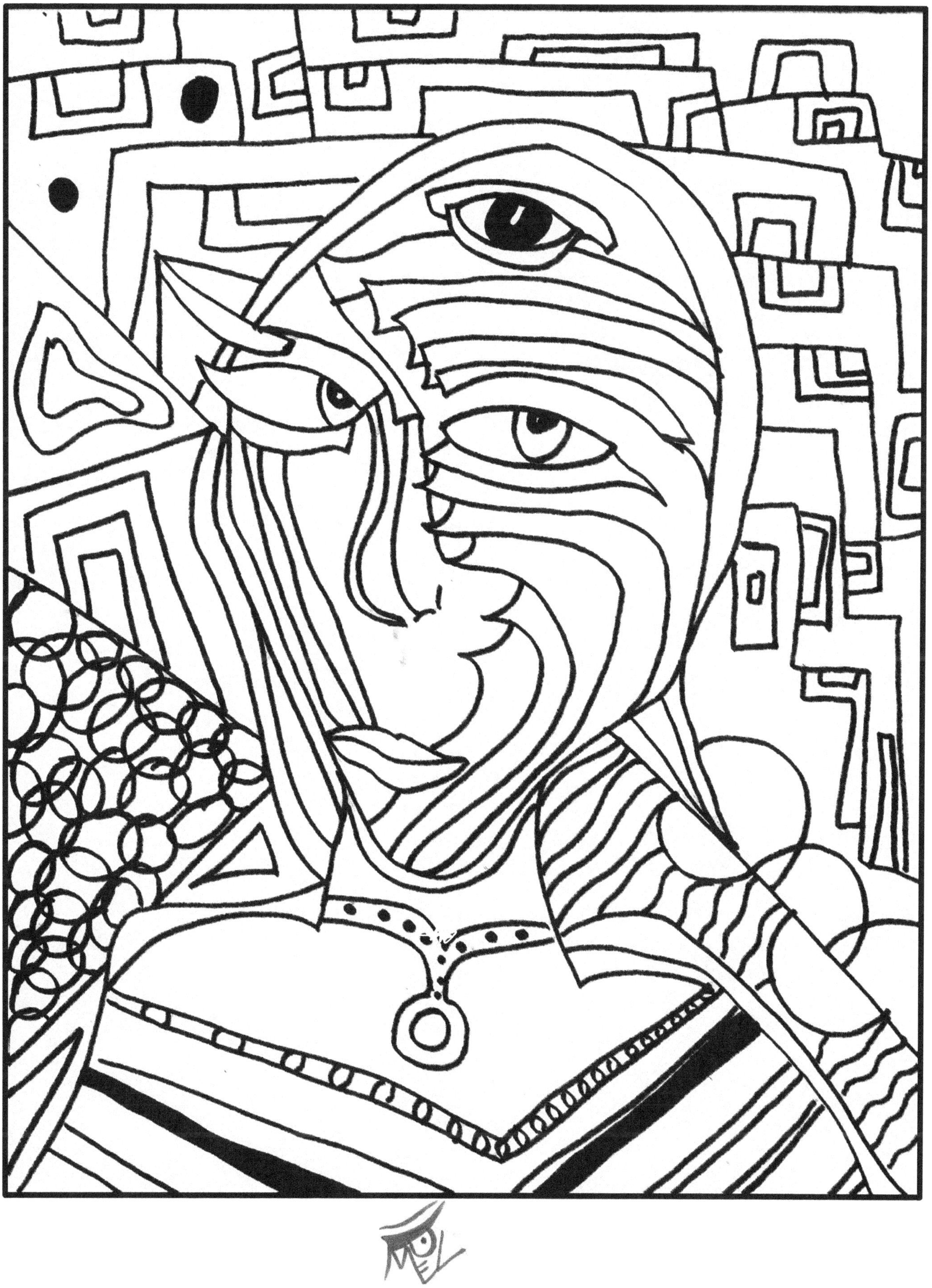

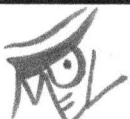

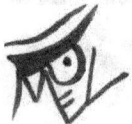

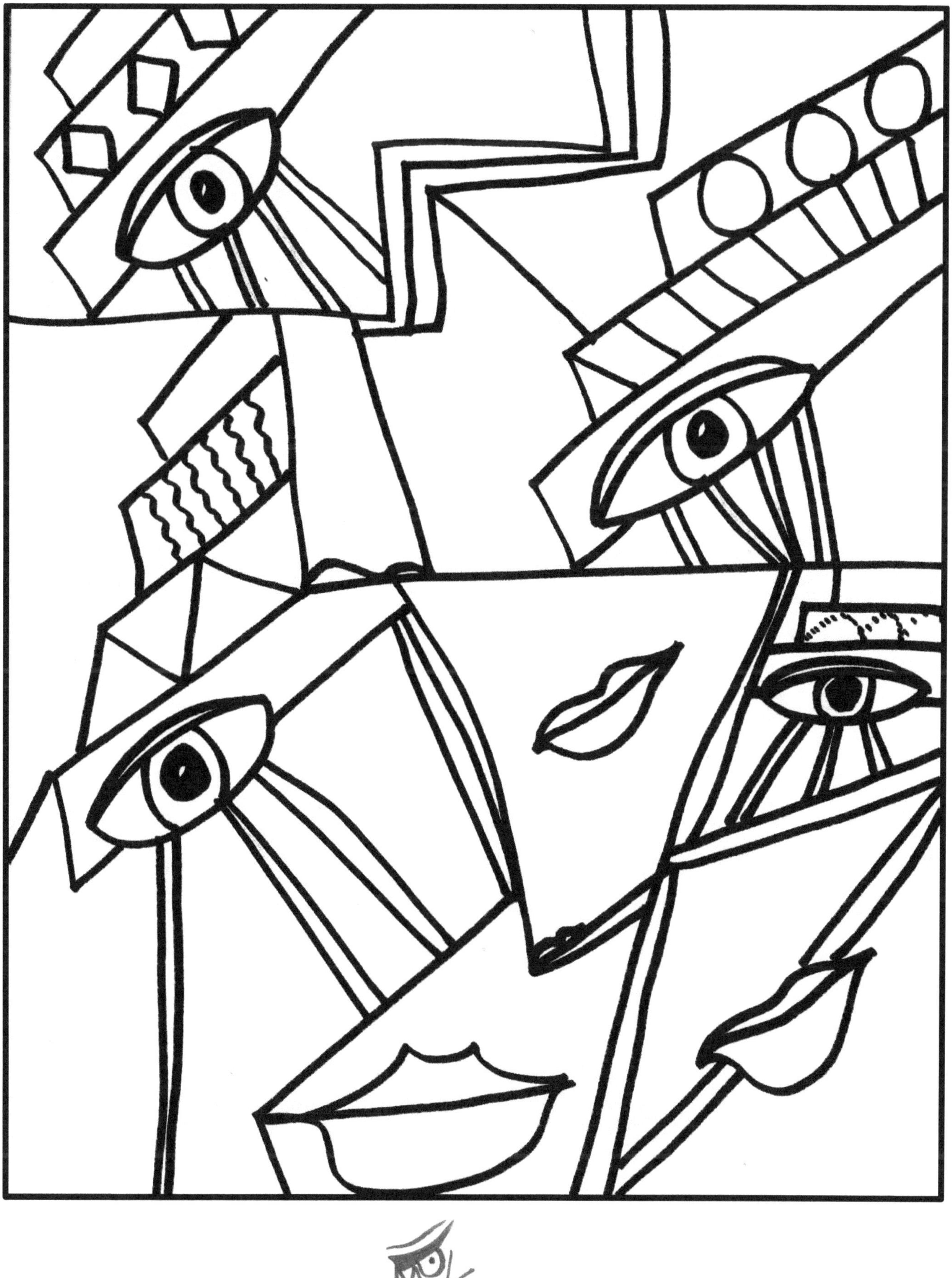

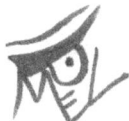

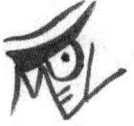

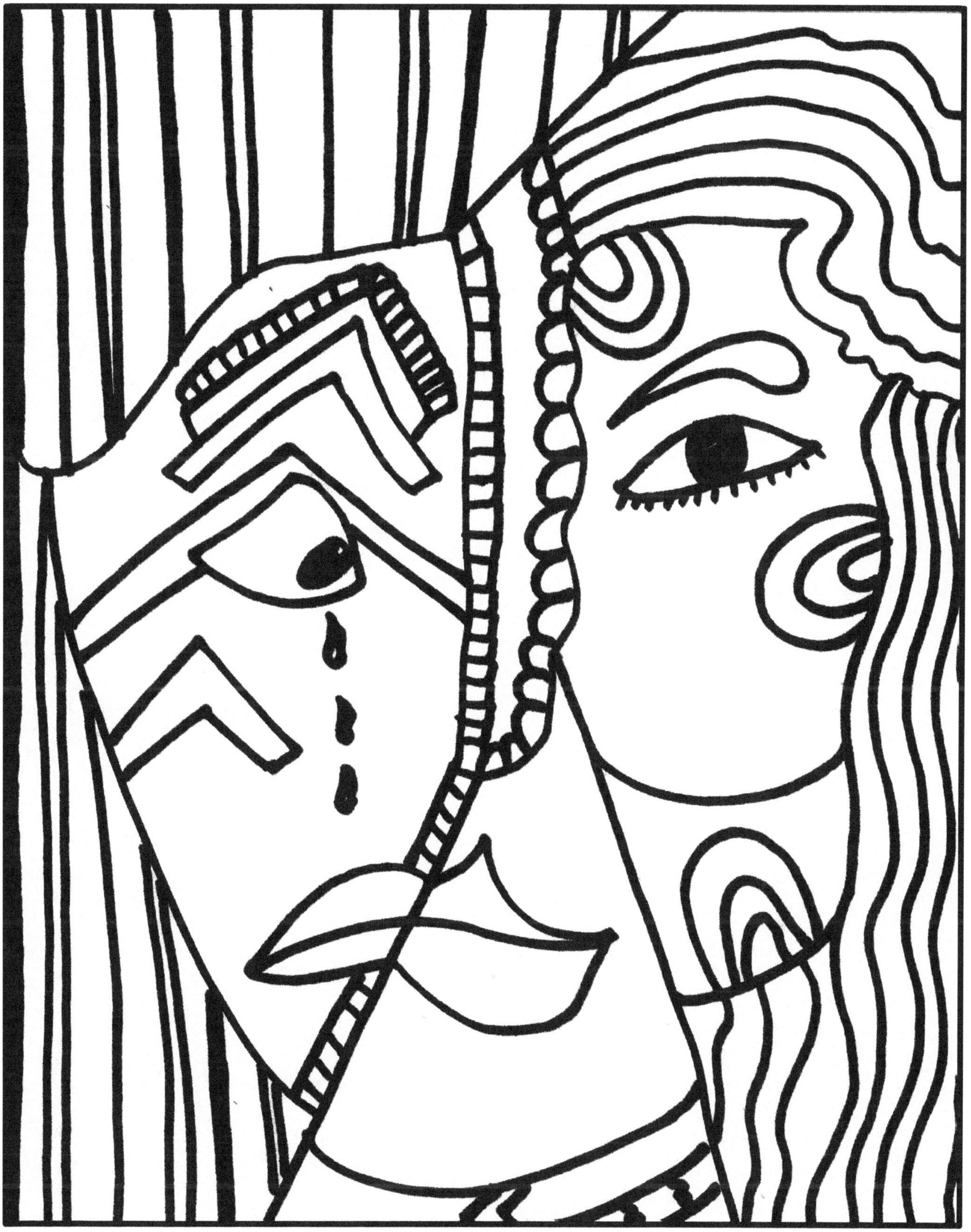

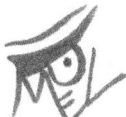

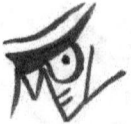

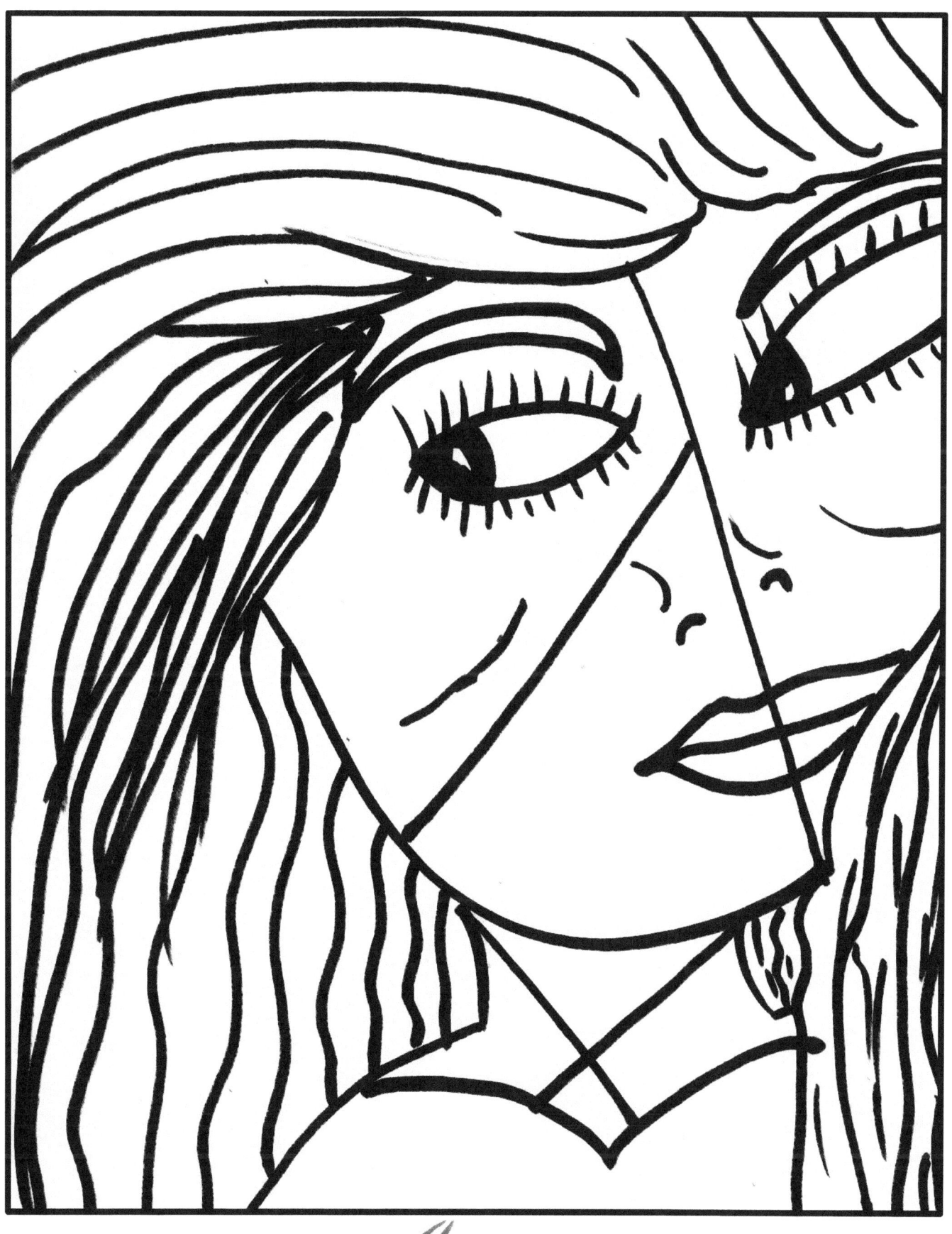

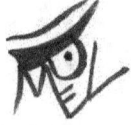

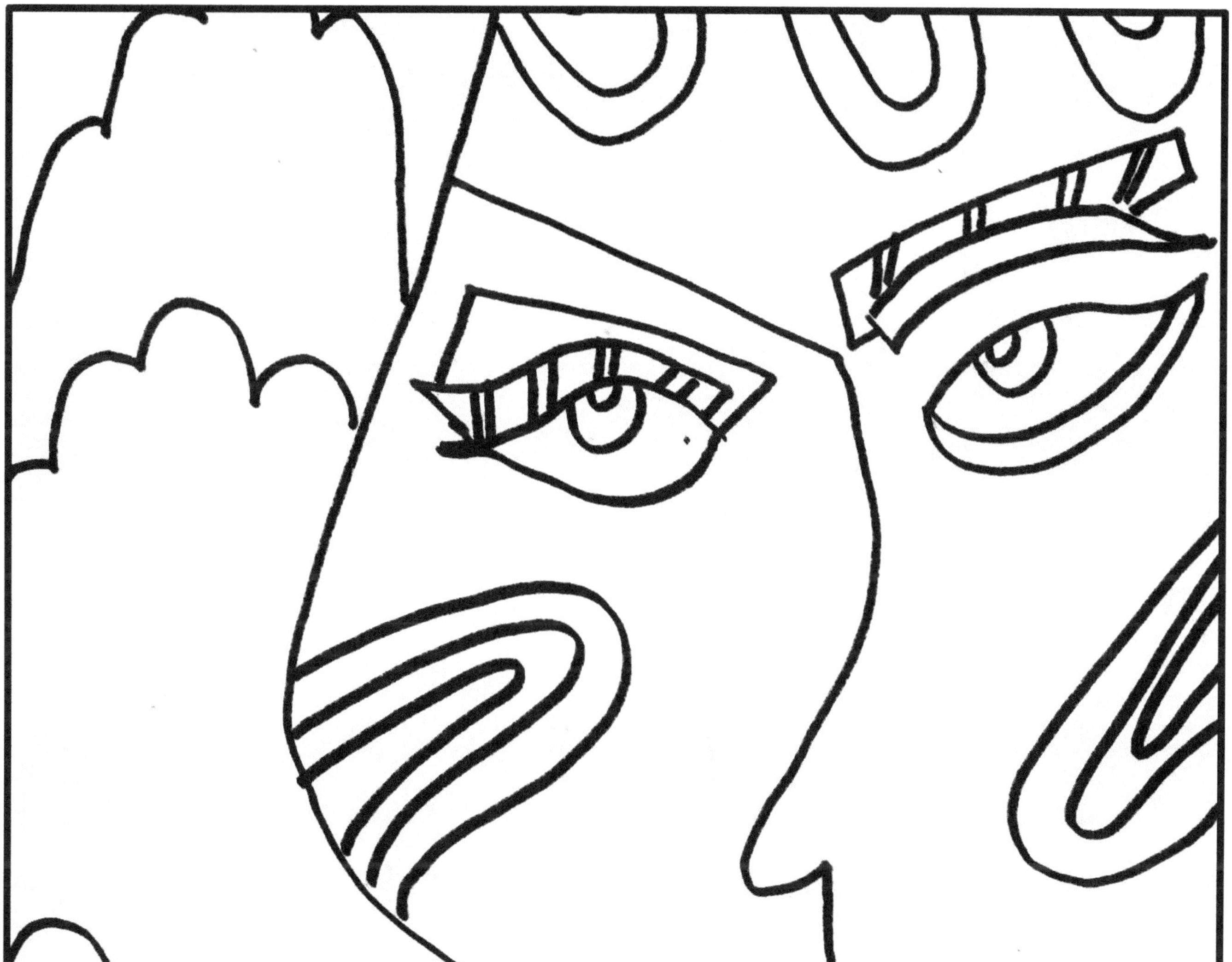

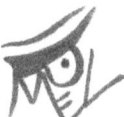

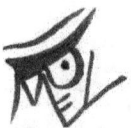

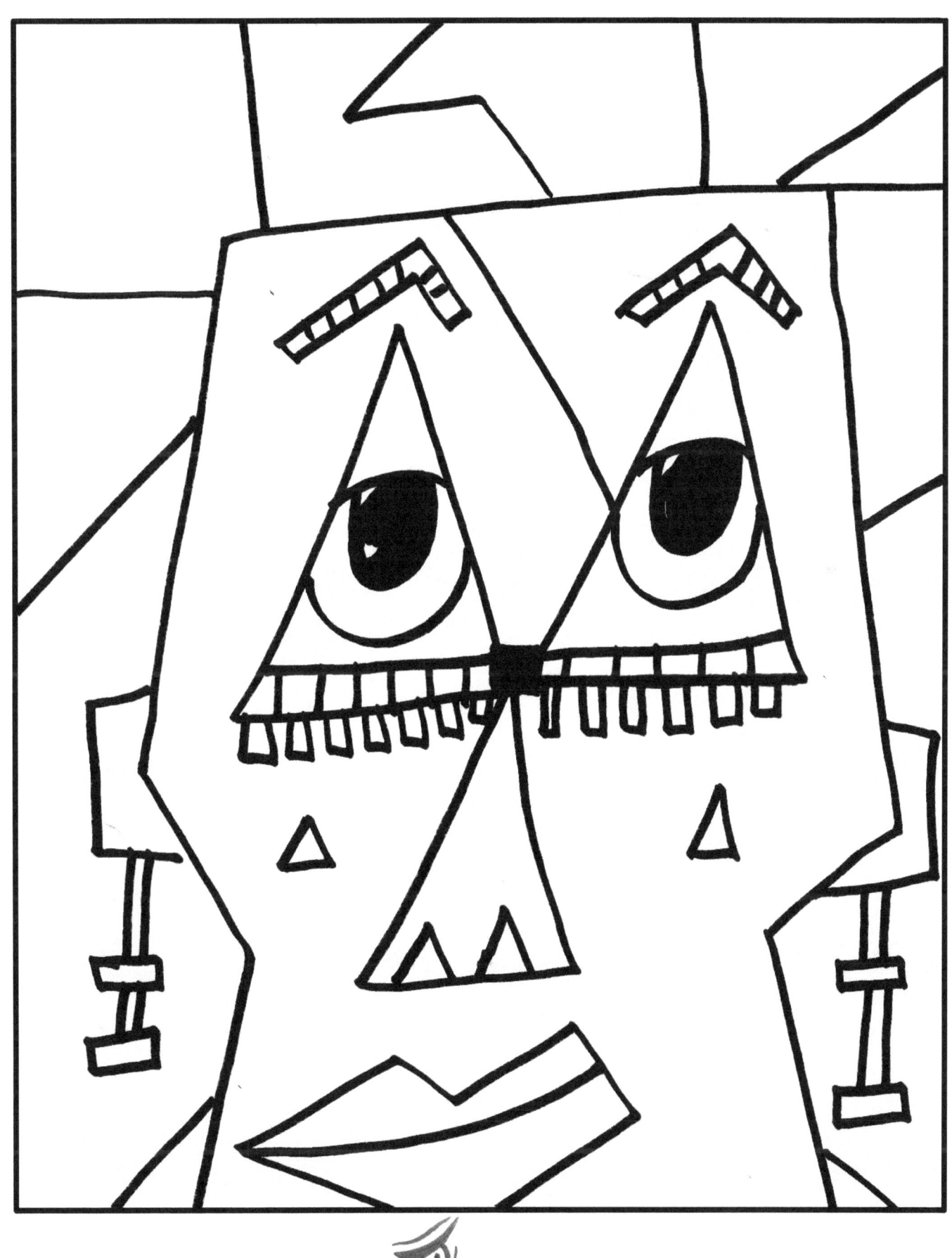

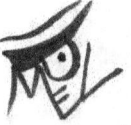

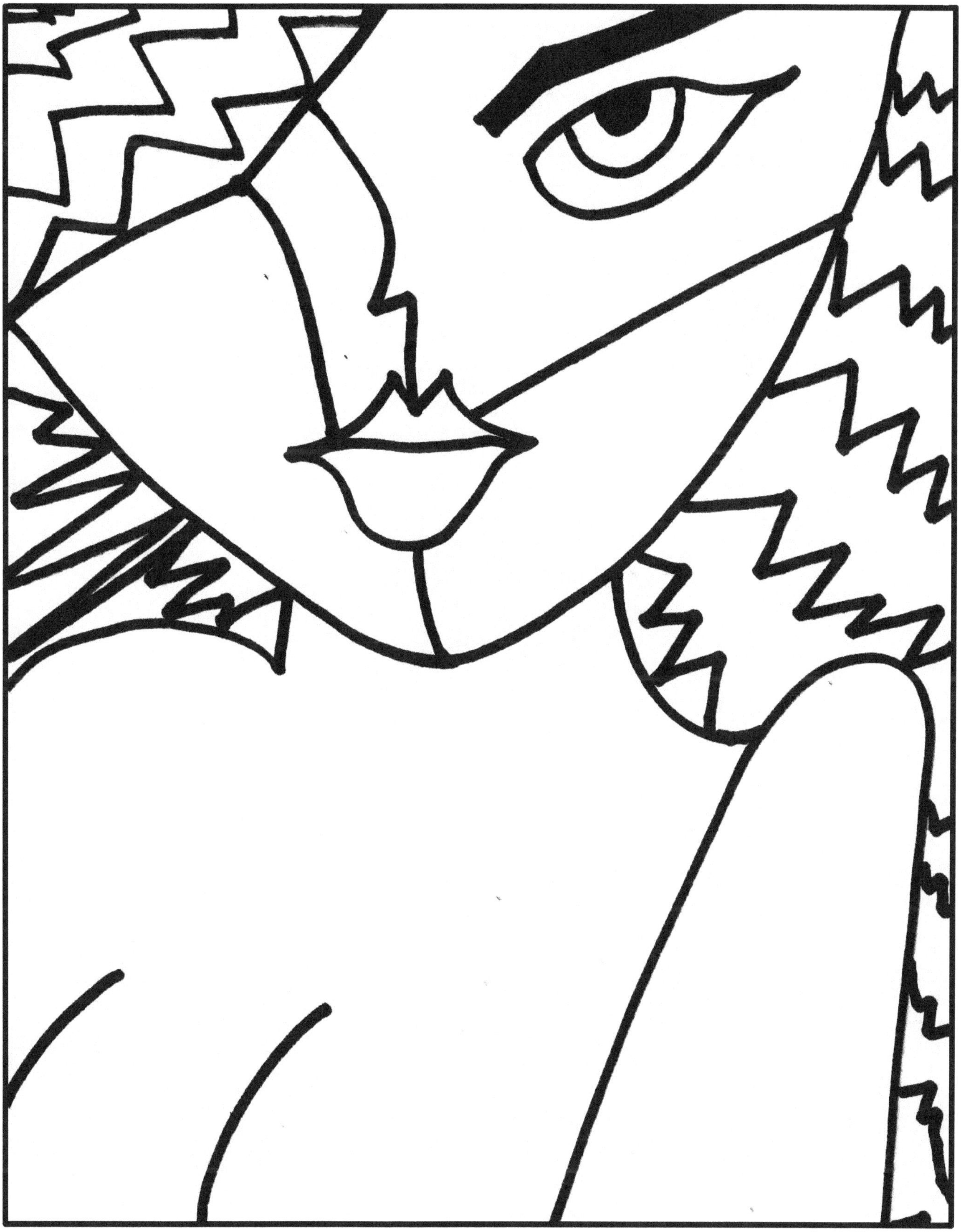

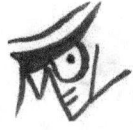

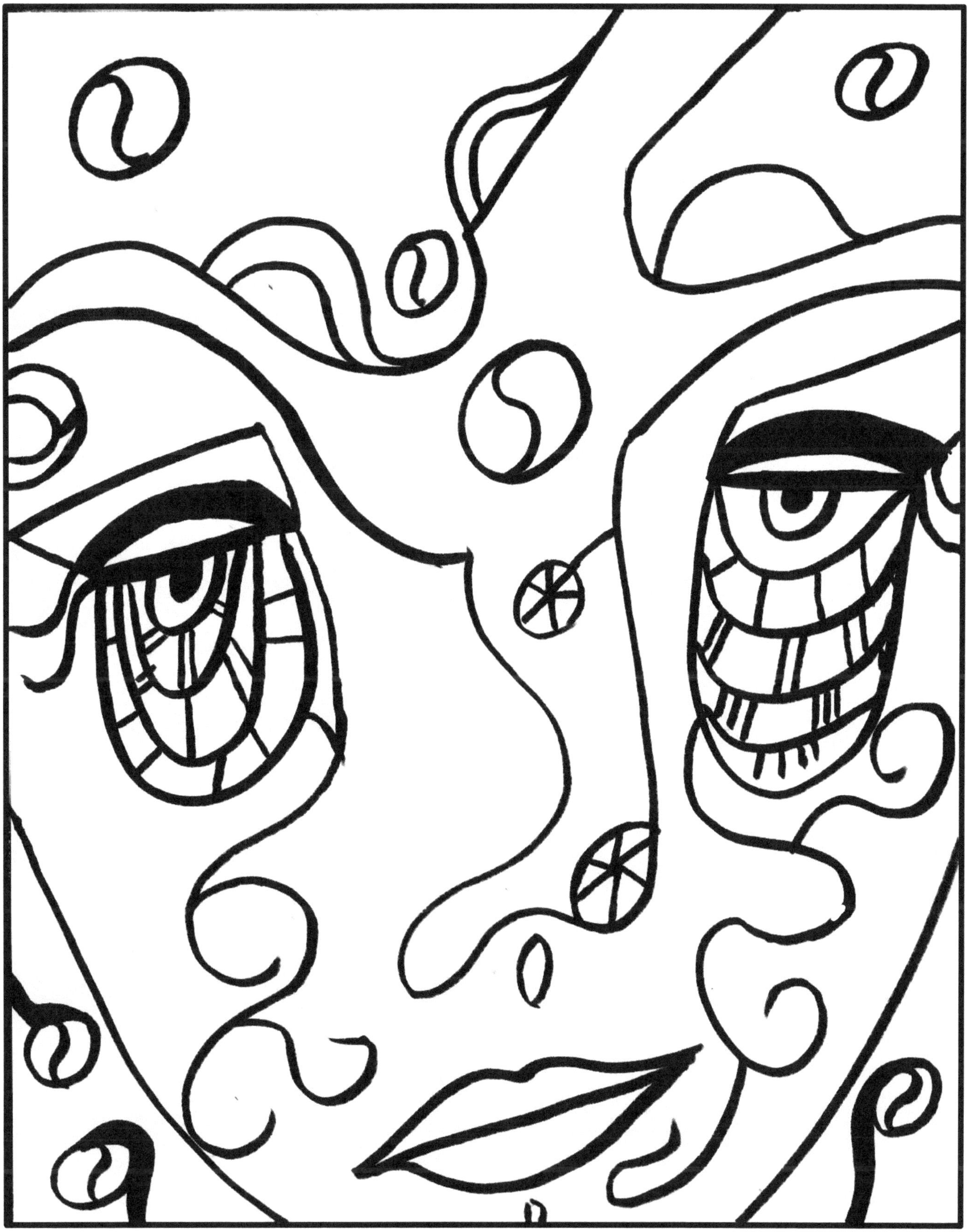

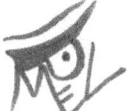

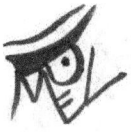

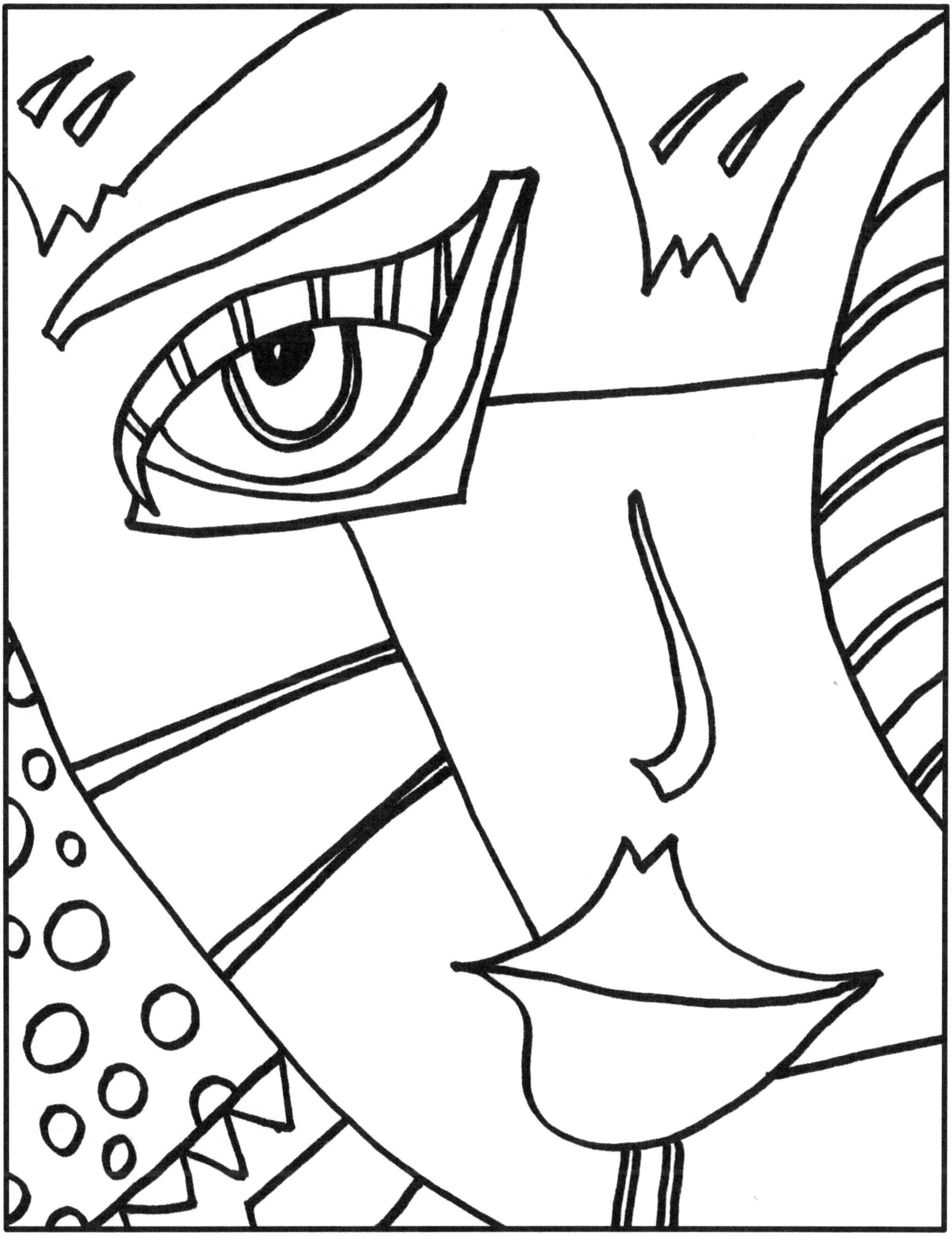

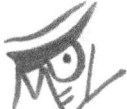

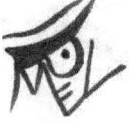

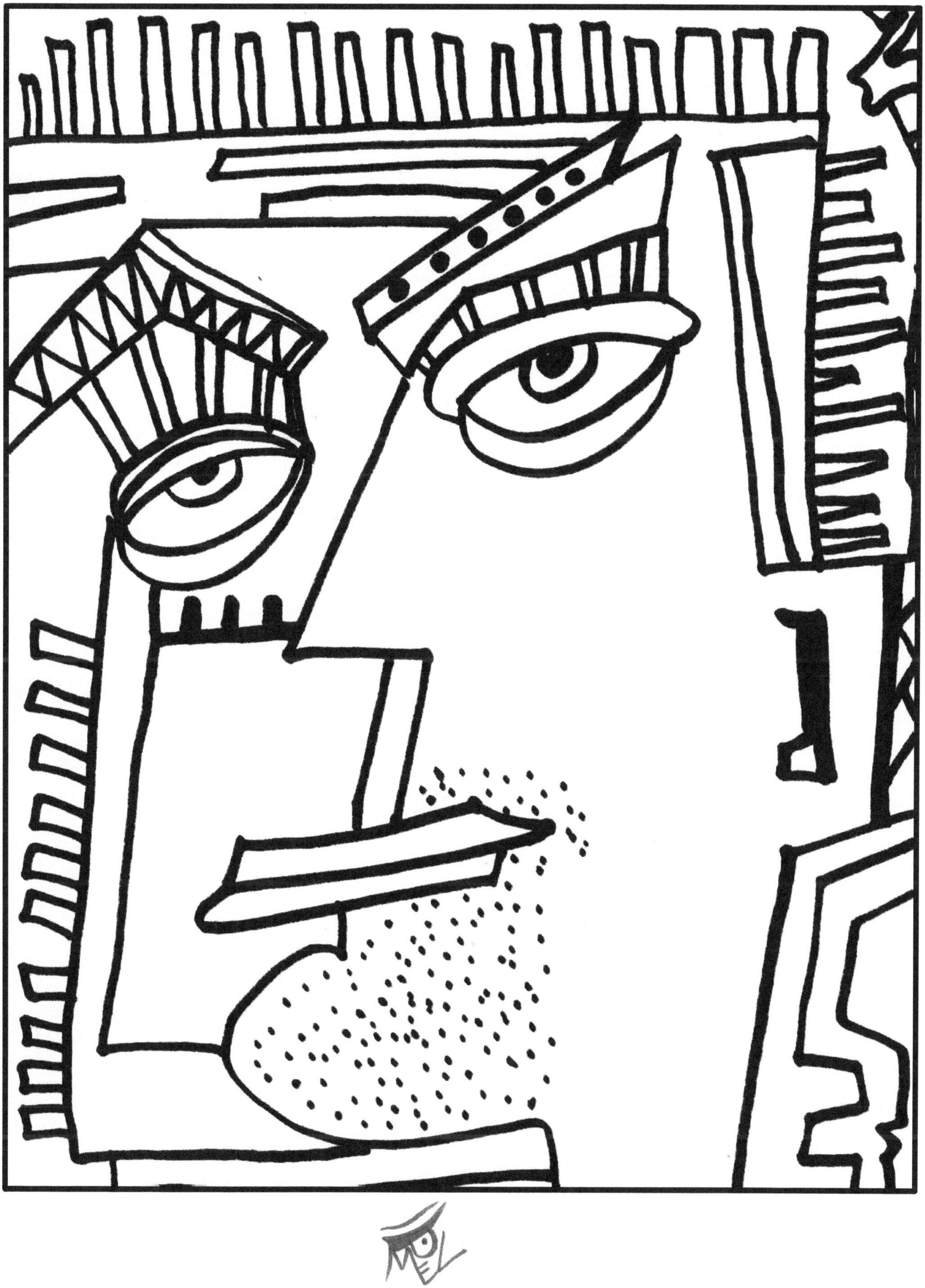

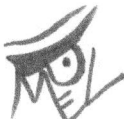

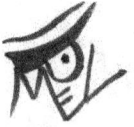

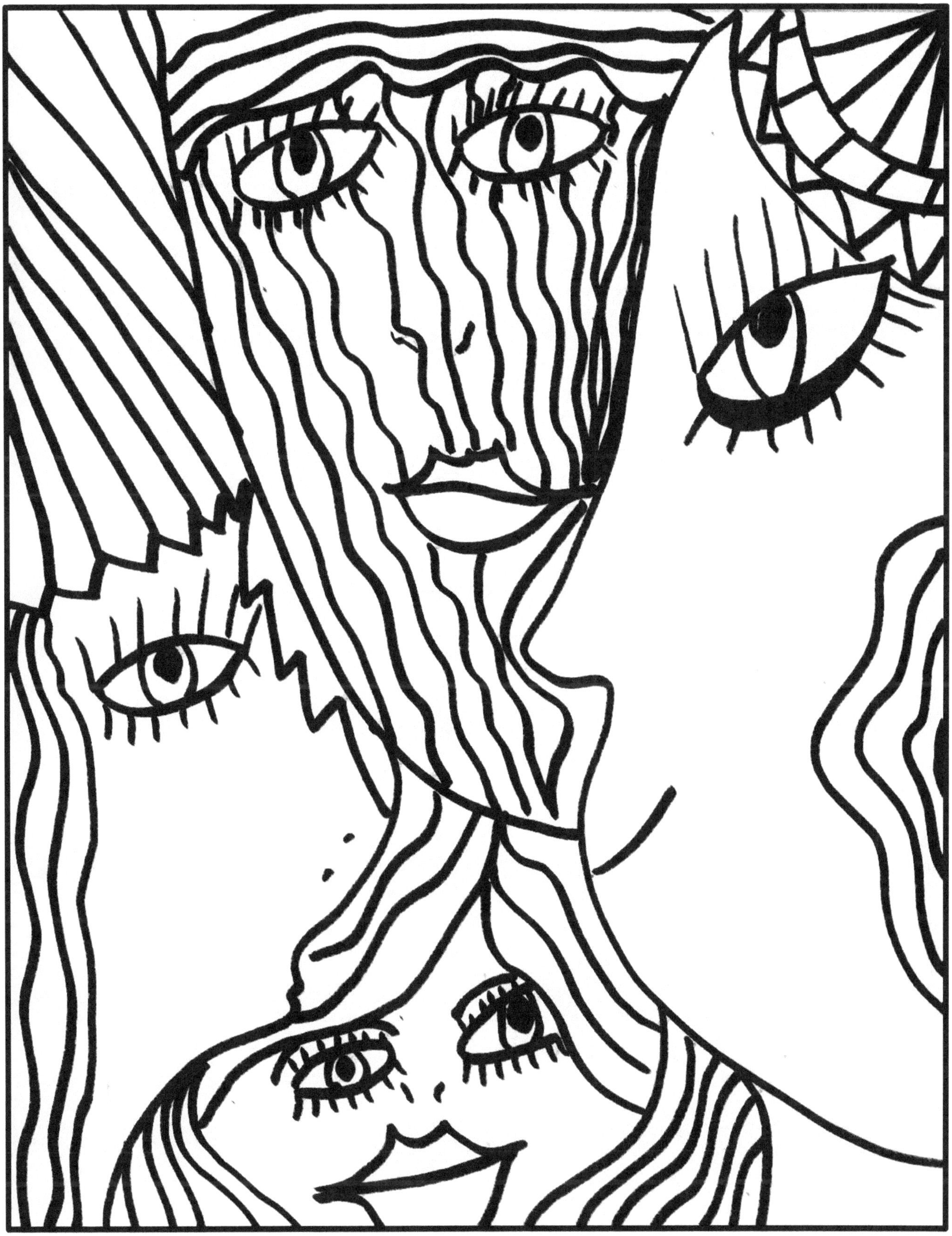

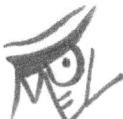

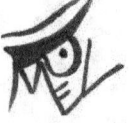

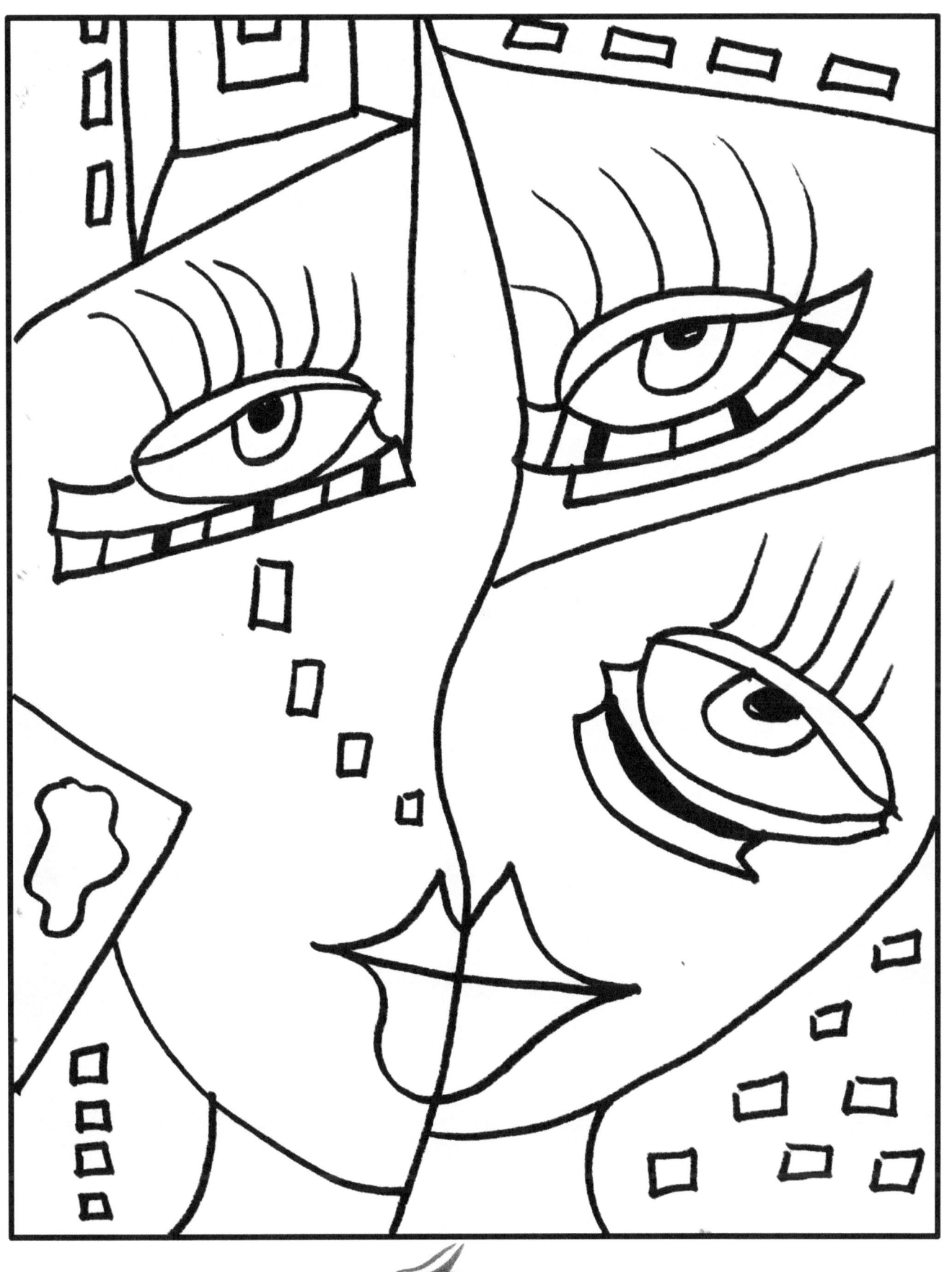

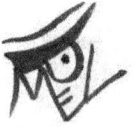

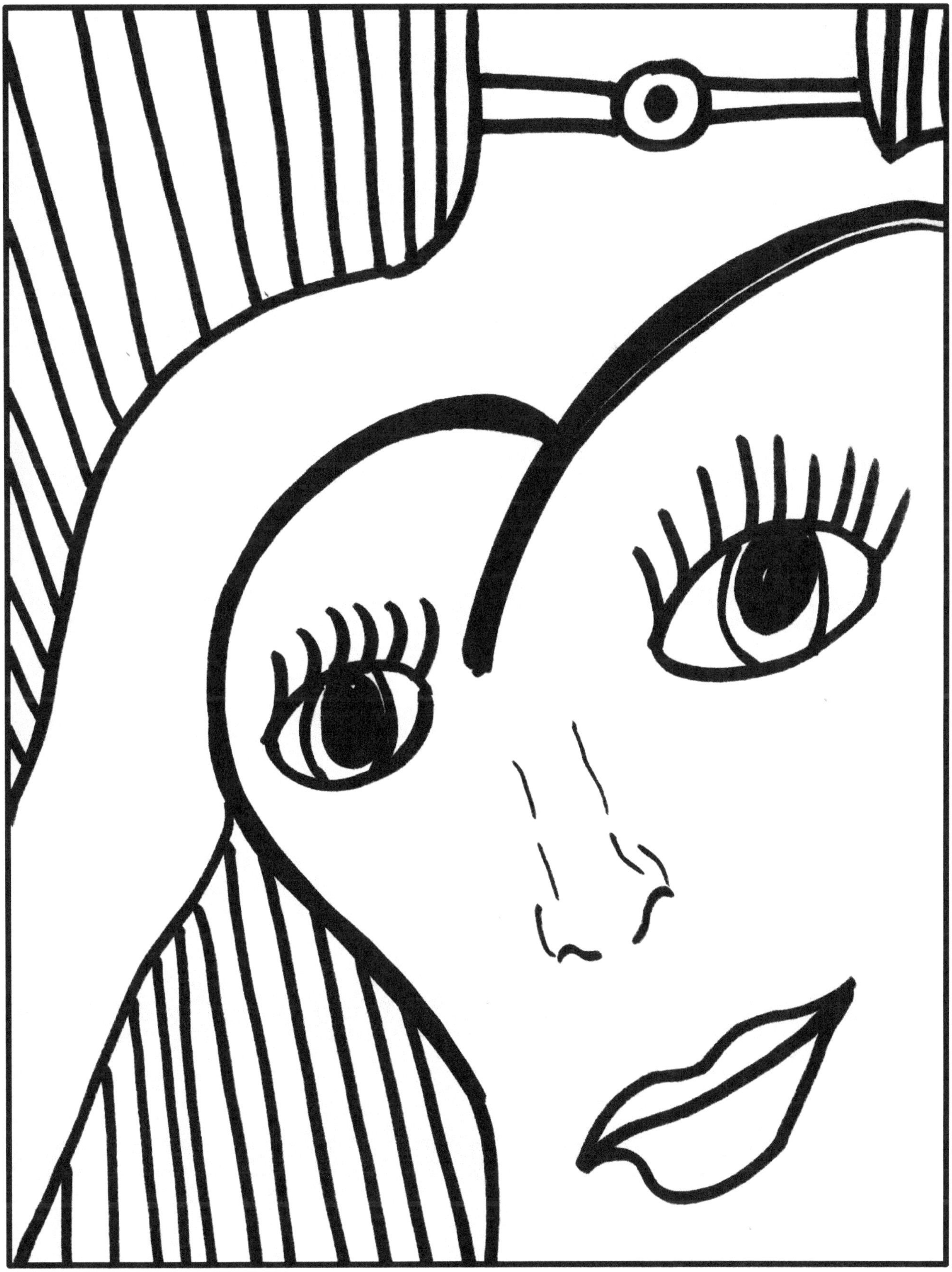

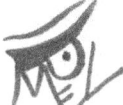

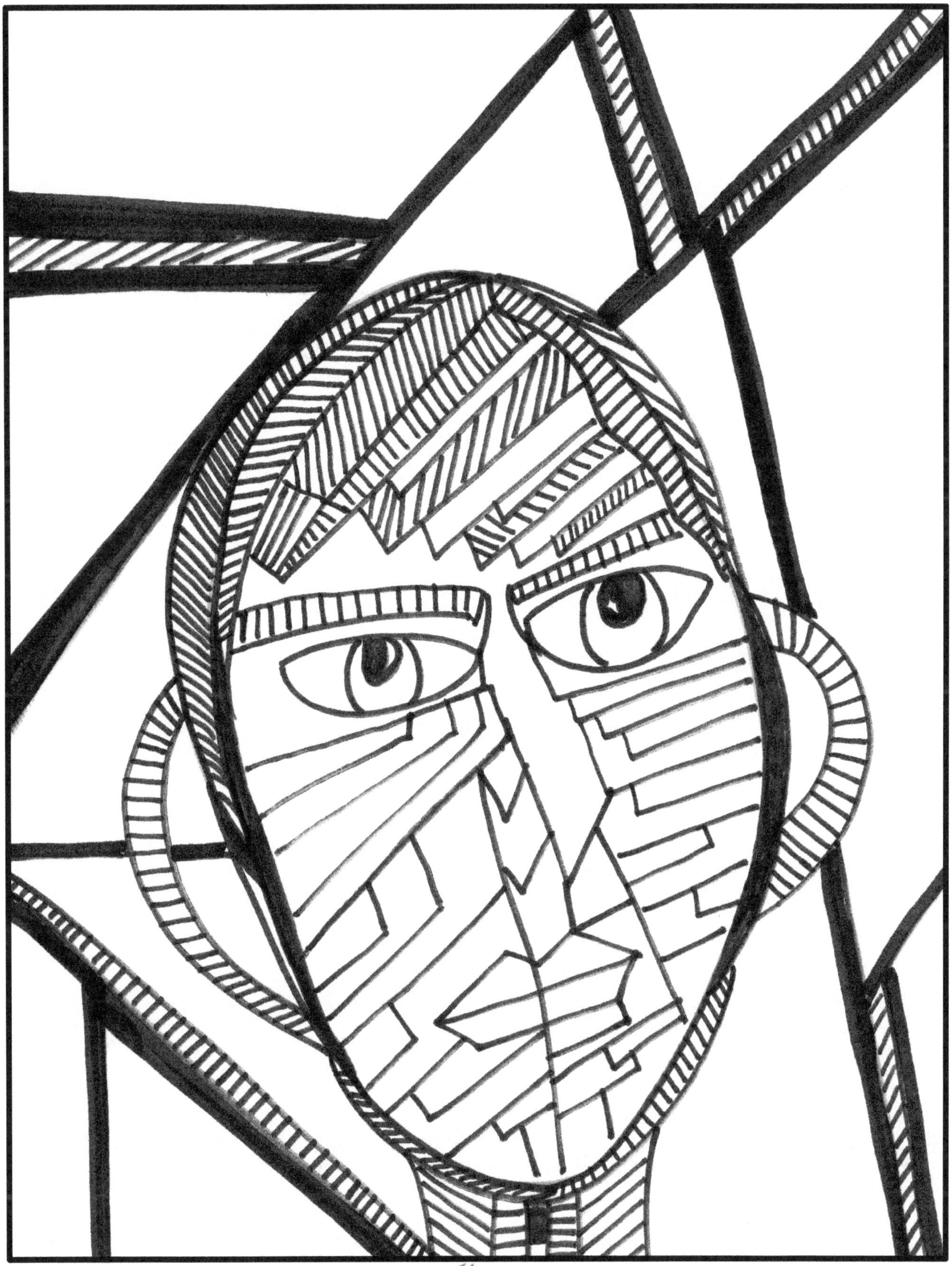

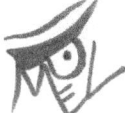

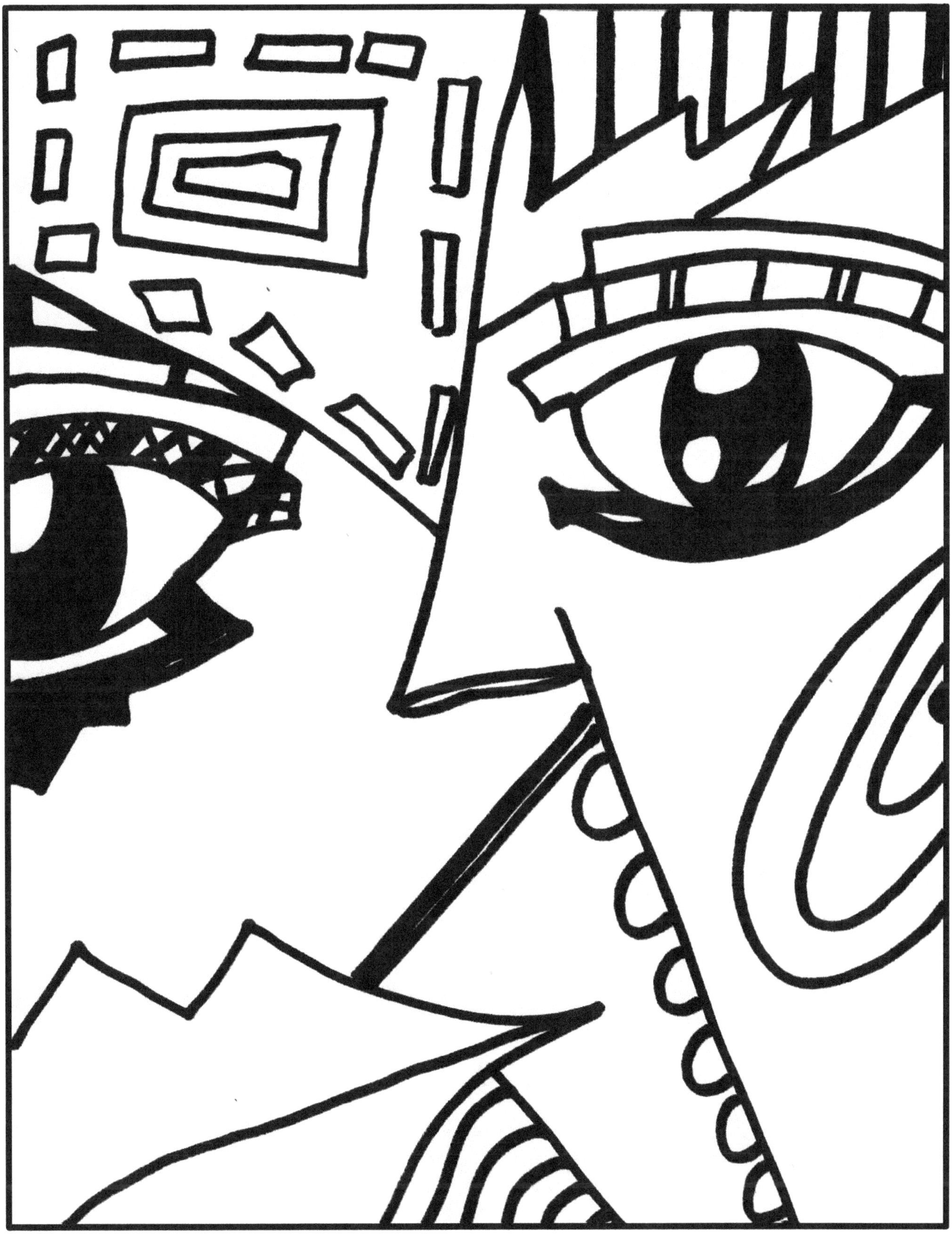

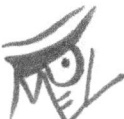

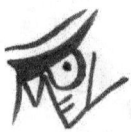

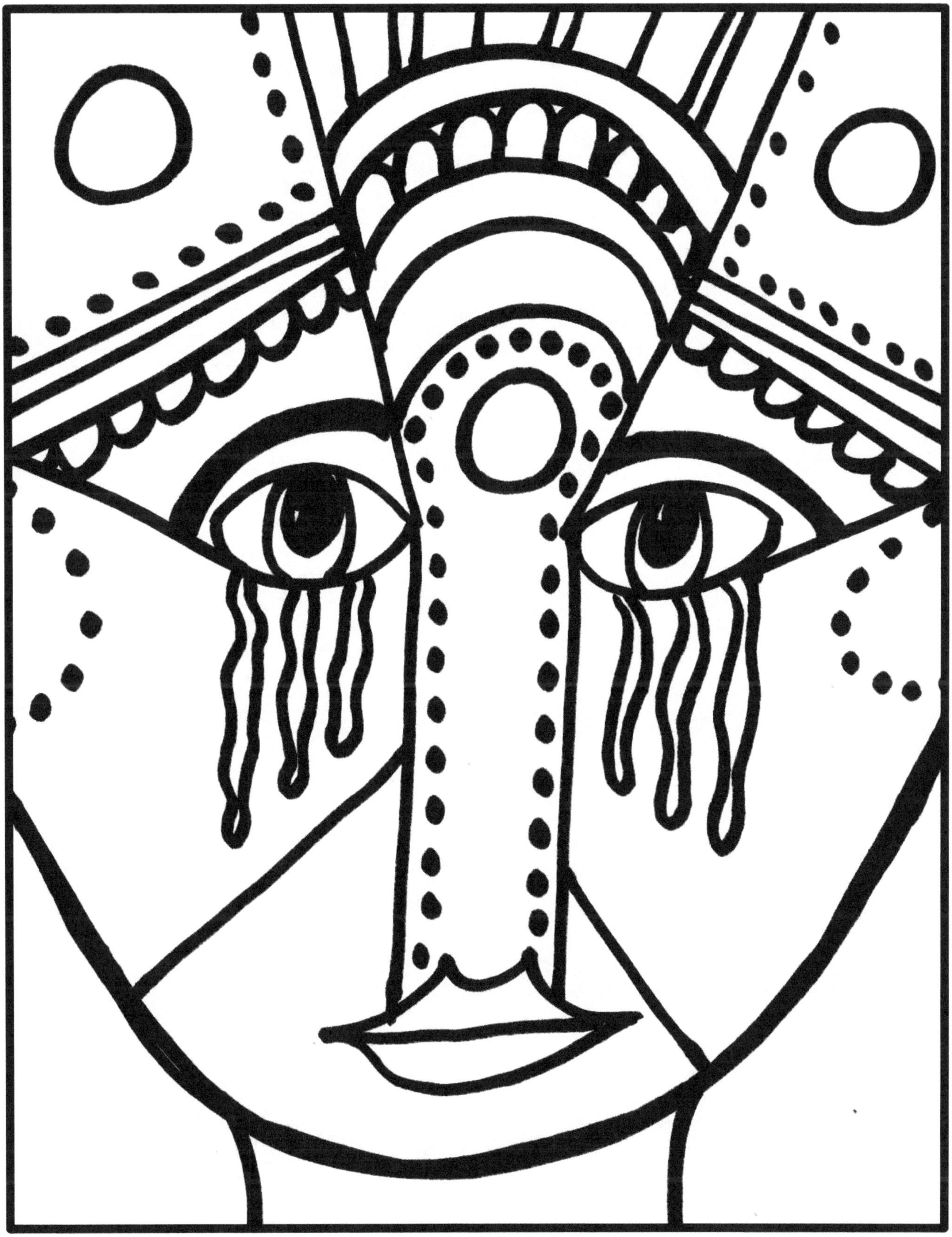

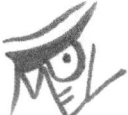

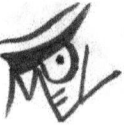

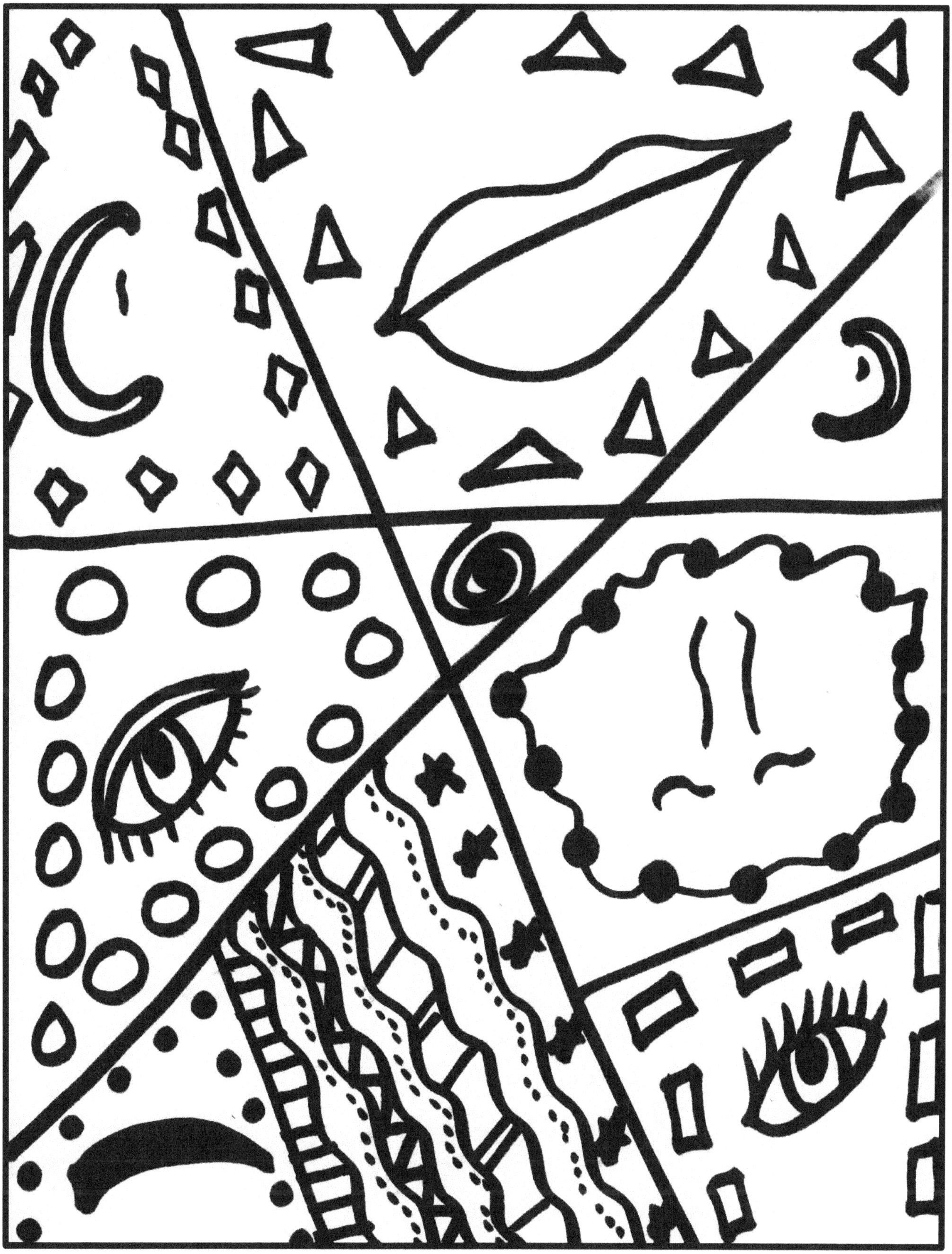

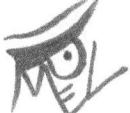

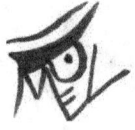

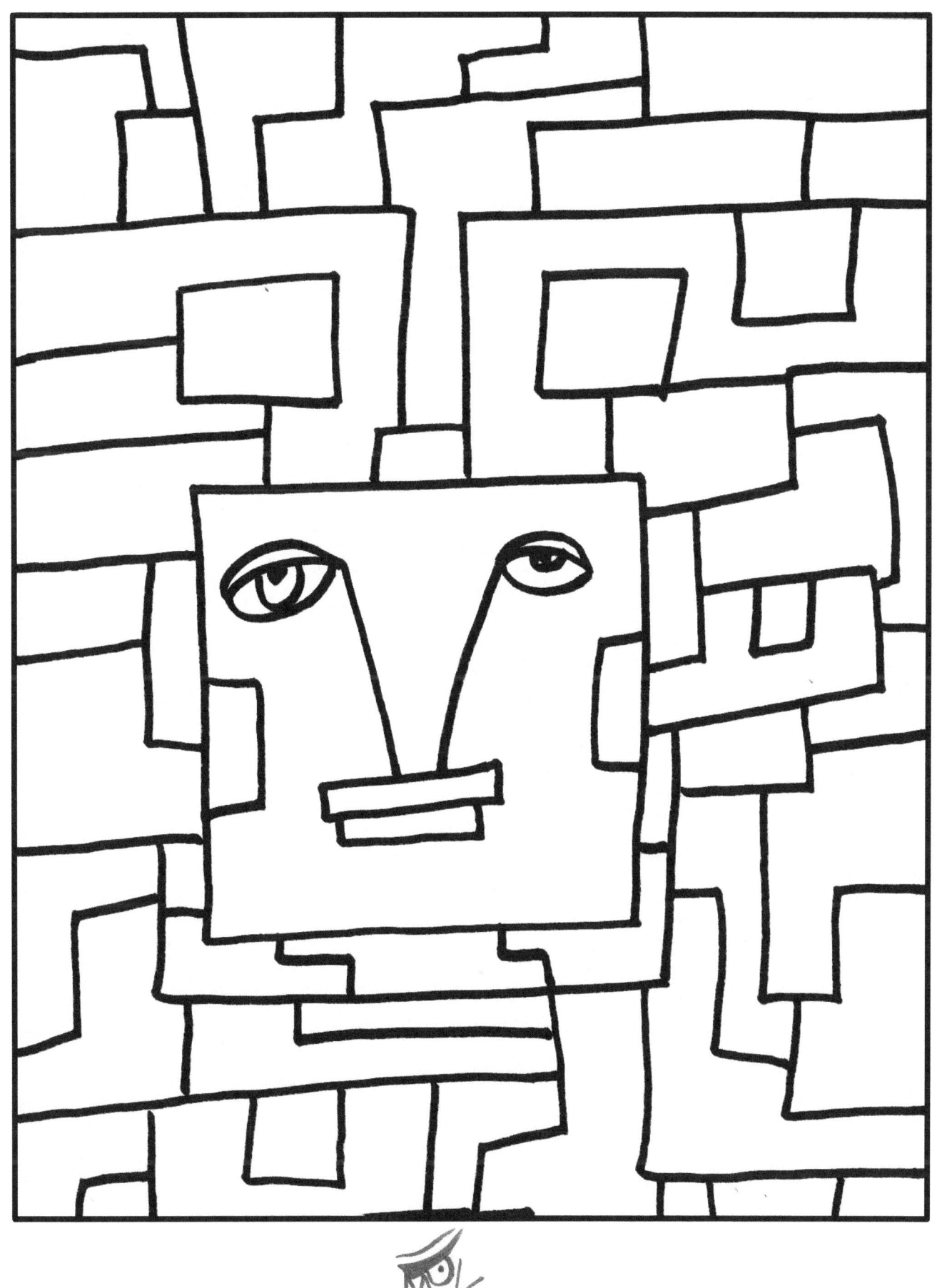

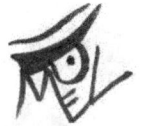

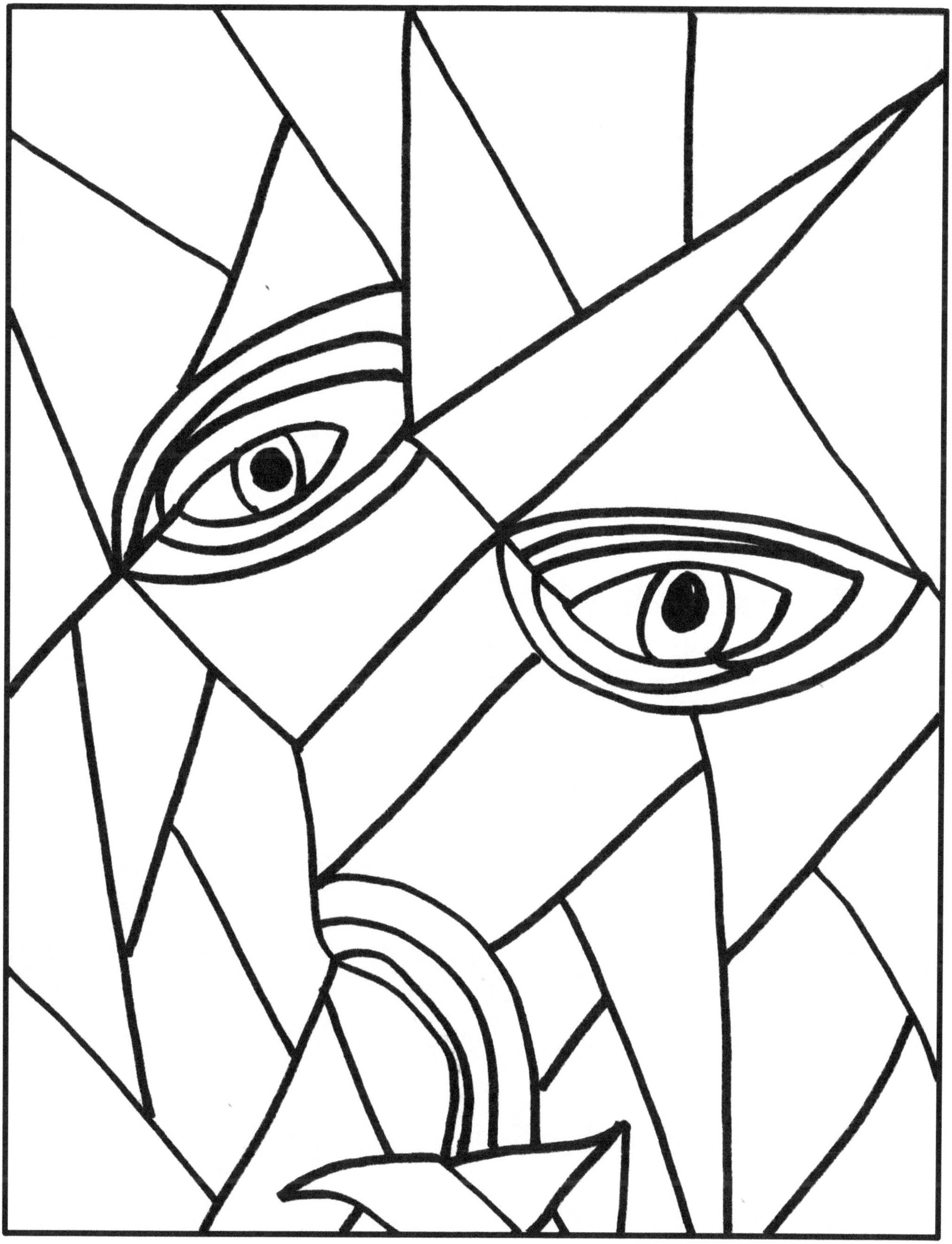

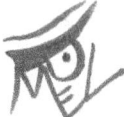

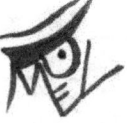

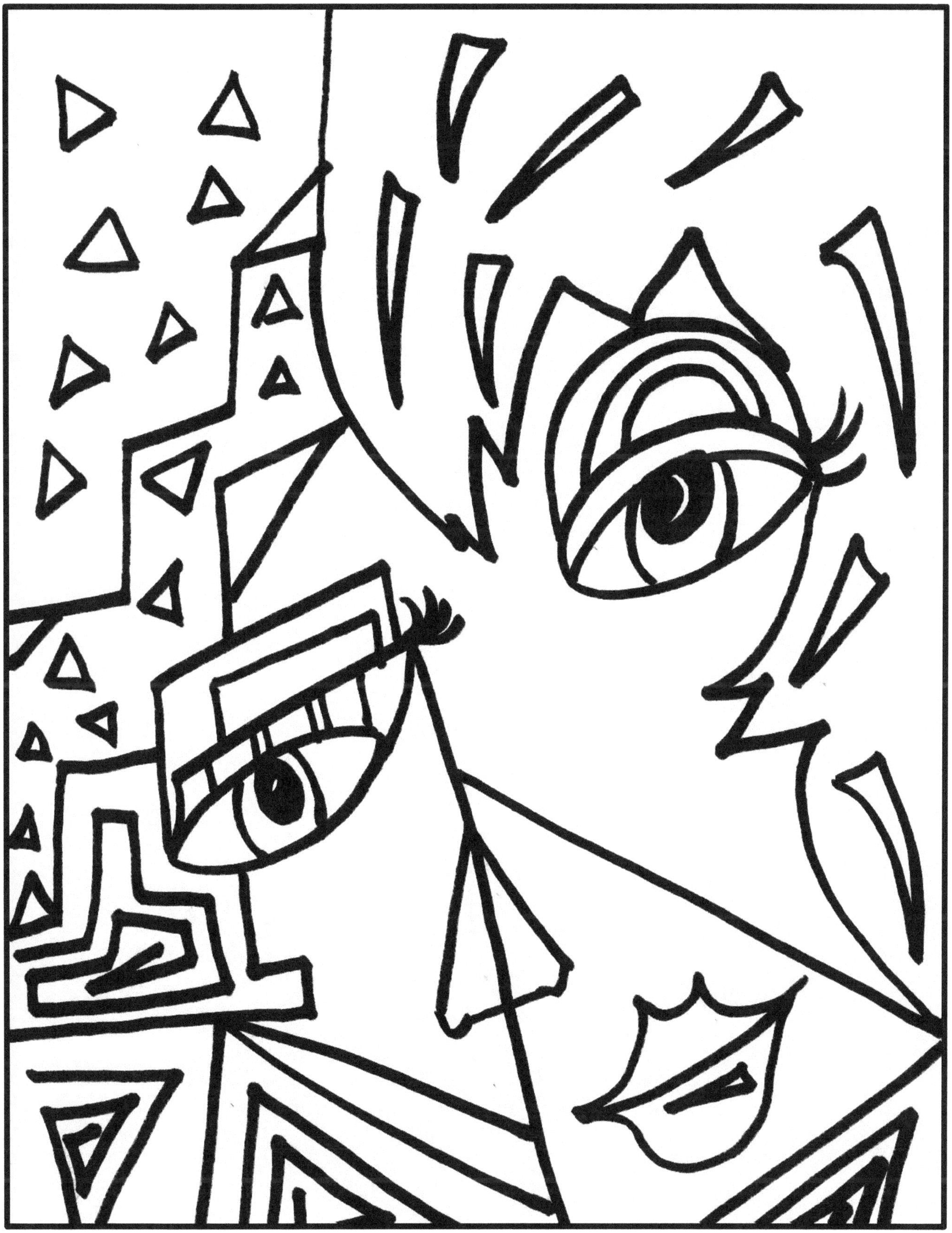

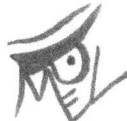

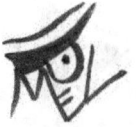

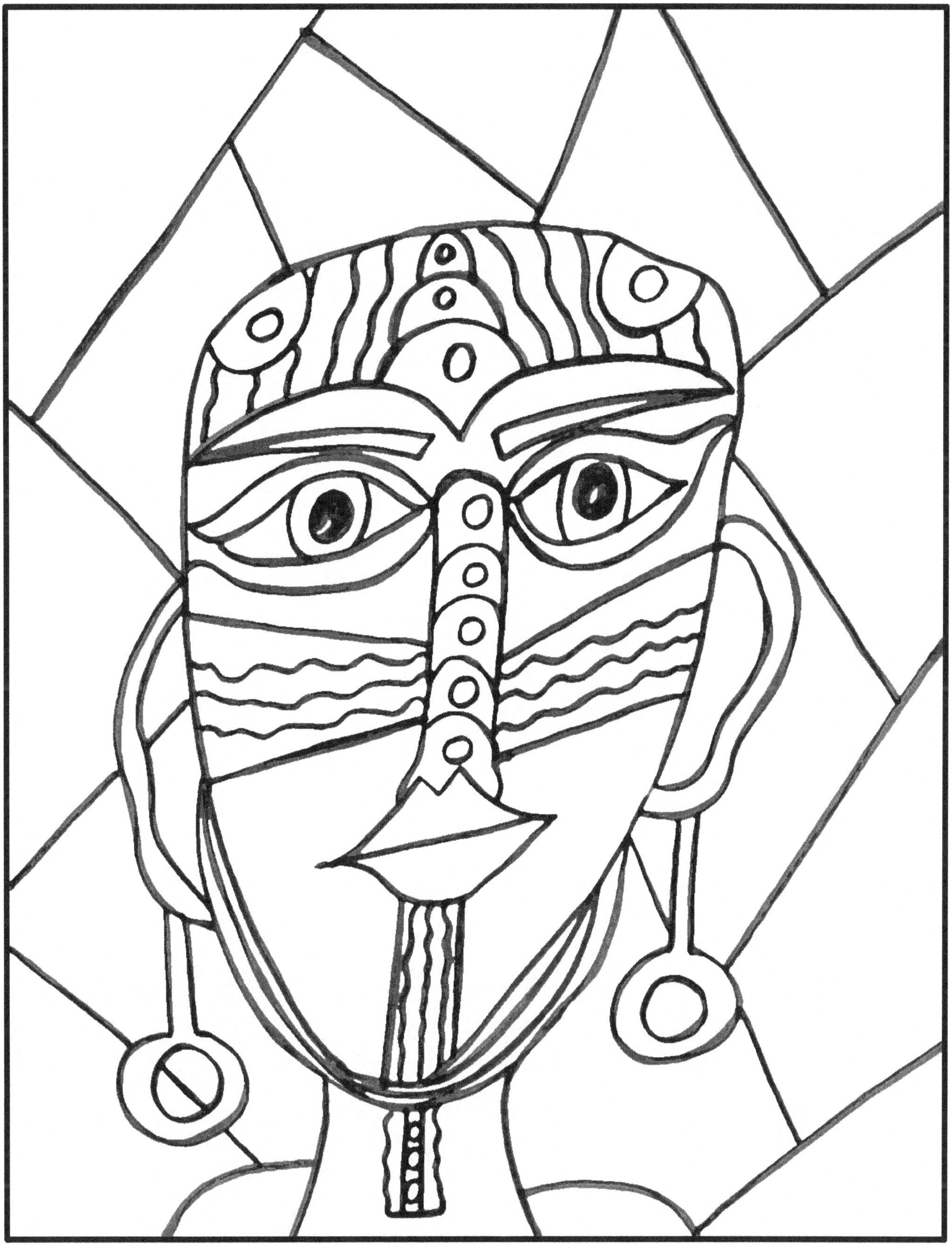

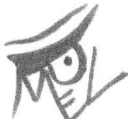

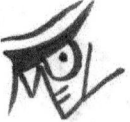

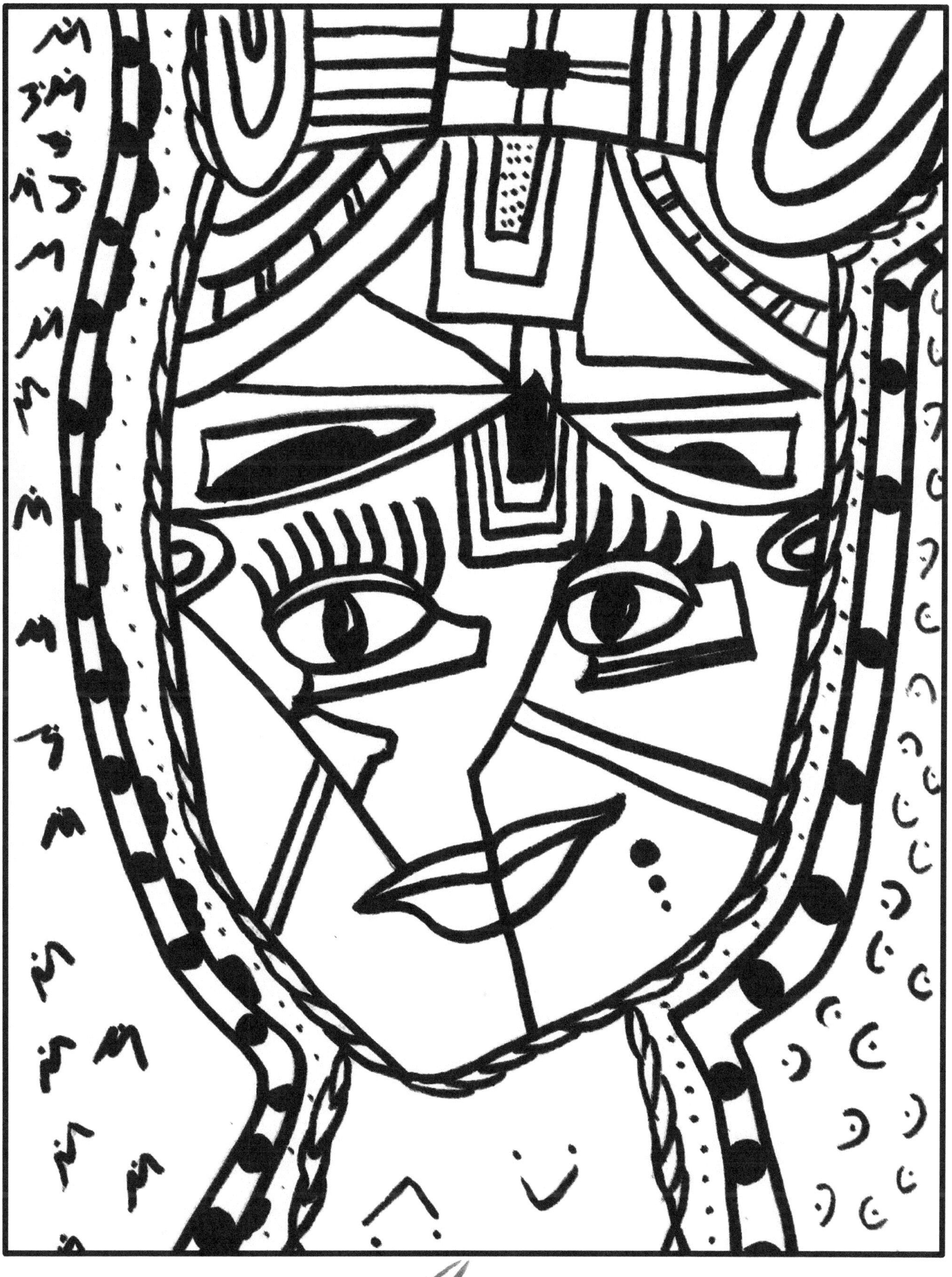

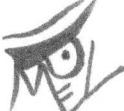

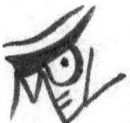

COLOR BLOCK SKETCH PAD

Not sure the color you chose will look good next to another? Use these blocks to test your colors before you use them on the drawings.

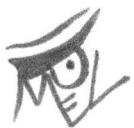

ADULT COLORING BOOKS BY MELISSA CAUDLE

Melissa Caudle has more adult coloring books available on Amazon, Barnes and Noble, and online retailers. You may also go to her website at:

www.drmelissacaudle.com

Abstract Faces Vols 1-5

Abstract Faces Carry Along Vol 1

Alien Faces Vols 1-2

Hippie Power

Cubism Faces

Pretty Faces

ORIGINAL ART BY MELISSA CAUDLE

Melissa Caudle sells her original art from her website: www.drmelissacaudle.com and on E-bay. Several of the original drawings included in this book, colored by the artist, may still be available for sale. They are a collector's item. All art is accompanied by a Certificate of Authenticity and signed by the artist.

CONTACT INFORMATION

Website: www.drmelissacaudle.com

Email: drmelcaudle@icloud.com   melabstractart@gmail.com

JOIN THE ABSTRACT FACES ADULT COLORING BOOK FACEBOOK SITE

Be sure to post your finished creations from the adult coloring books by Melissa Caudle and share in the fun on the above website. I can wait to see your creations.

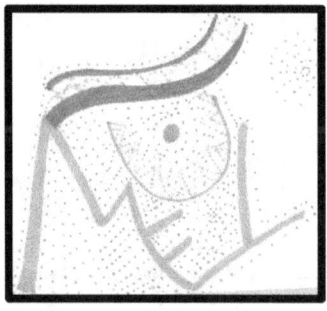